Renewing Your Ministry

Renewing Your Ministry

*Walking With Jesus
in All That You Do*

Joe Paprocki

ave maria press   Notre Dame, IN

International Standard Book Number: 0-87793-941-1
Cover design by Brian C. Conley
Text design by Brian C. Conley
Printed and bound in the United States of America.

Library of Congress Cataloging-in-Publication Data
Paprocki, Joe.
    Renewing your ministry : walking with Jesus in all that you do / Joe Paprocki.
        p. cm.
    ISBN 0-87793-941-1 (pbk.)
    1. Pastoral theology--Catholic Church. 2. Spiritual life--Catholic Church. I. Title.
BX1913 .P275   2000
248.4'82--dc21   00-008463
                                                            CIP

For my Jo.
The Lord opens my eyes
and I'm blessed to have you fill them
each and every day.

Special thanks to the following: to the two Tom's in my life, Tom McLaughlin and my brother Tom for helping me locate a particularly difficult-to-find scripture passage about God spitting; again to Tom M. for letting me borrow from his library and for a wonderful and inspirational morning on Lake Tampier near his old family farm; to Joe Sodini for teaching me to let go, ride a bicycle and ice skate; to the staff of St. Elizabeth Seton Parish in Orland Hills for allowing me to walk with them on the road to Emmaus and for allowing me to test new material on them; to my dad and my Uncle Joe for my apprenticeship; to Bob and Michelle Mangold for a week in rainy, snowy Arizona that somehow indirectly inspired this book; and to Jim Campbell for blessing my bookshelves with a copy of the *NJBC* at just the right time. Oh, and thanks to the Chicago Cubs for repeatedly lifting and dashing my hopes during the last 40 years of the twentieth century. I am stronger for it. This millennium will be better . . . I can feel it!

Contents

Introduction

It's no coincidence that the idea for *Renewing Your Ministry: Walking With Jesus in All That You Do* came to me while I was walking on a treadmill. I had just returned from a ten day spring vacation in Arizona with my wife Joanne and our two kids, Mike and Amy. It had been a long, cold Chicago winter and we all had been looking forward to getting away to the warmth of Arizona. I was looking to overcome some slight writer's block accompanied by general malaise and figured the warm and sunny southwest would be the cure. Unfortunately, the weather in Arizona never got above 65 degrees, it rained four of the ten days we were there, and it actually snowed once! Luckily for us, we did get to see the majesty of Sedona and the Grand Canyon but no magical inspiration for a new book or bolt of energy came to revive me.

Arriving back home to Chicago, depression quickly set in as we returned to gray skies, 40 degrees, rain, and the prospect of going back to school and work. To get my mind off of things, I went where I usually go . . . to the health club for a run. As I was running, it occurred to me how ironic it was to be running on the treadmill since the prospect of going back to work the next day meant getting back on the treadmill of life. It meant, literally, getting back on the road again—the Dan Ryan expressway to be exact. It was *at that moment*, not on the glorious hills and mountains of Arizona and the Grand Canyon, but while running on a treadmill at the health club on 87th and Kedzie and watching the Cubs lose their third game in a row (with Sammy Sosa striking out for the ninth time in 18 at bats thrown into the mix) that the inspiration for this book came to me.

As I thought about the prospect of going back to work the next day, the image of the two disciples on the road to Emmaus (Lk 24:13-35) popped into my head. How trivial my concerns seemed in comparison to the pain those two disciples experienced, and yet Jesus walked with them and found a way to transform their lives! Certainly he could transform my life as well! The more I thought about the road to Emmaus story, the more I realized that we need not go to the Grand Canyon or the top of a mountain to find the risen Lord. We can encounter him on a treadmill at the health club, or on the Dan Ryan expressway, or on a dusty road to a nowhere-town called Emmaus.

Like those two disciples, we often find ourselves in need of renewal—maybe mired in despair and malaise, suffering from a loss of inspiration, idealism, vision, energy, and mission. The bottom line is that our ministry is in need of renewal! Christ is risen and walking right alongside of us, yet somehow, we seem to be unable or unwilling to recognize him. We cannot see the new life in our midst because we are too busy looking at all the negatives.

My goal in writing *Renewing Your Ministry: Walking With Jesus in All That You Do* is to provide a framework for pastoral ministers to assess their personal spiritual direction, recapture a sense of idealism, and recommit themselves to their ministry. As pastoral ministers, we too find ourselves often needing a new start, a new way to envision our same ministry. We've been around the block more than a few times. We've been there and done that and sometimes it seems like everything we had once been so excited about has somehow slowly slipped away from us. We find ourselves going through the motions of our ministry, walking on the treadmill of the liturgical or catechetical year but not recognizing the risen Lord in our midst.

In the scripture story, however, an amazing thing happens to those two disciples: their eyes are opened and they come to recognize the risen Jesus! Before long, they are doing a 180 degree turn and heading back to Jerusalem . . . on the same road again but this time with renewed energy and vision. From Jerusalem, the road is called the *road to Emmaus*. If you're in Emmaus, however, the same road is called the *road to Jerusalem*. Same road, but one direction leads to nowhere while the other leads to the dwelling place of the all-powerful, ever-living God. It's the place of Calvary, an empty tomb, an upper room where brothers and sisters await the return of missing disciples, and best of all, it's the place of new life.

The story of the two disciples on the road to Emmaus provides pastoral ministers with a framework for profound spiritual and ministerial growth. After the death of Jesus, two disciples are journeying on the road to Emmaus, shrouded in despair, confusion, and loss of idealism, unaware of the resurrection. Their mysterious encounter with the risen Jesus on the road transforms their lives and renews their commitment to discipleship and ministry. In the same way, pastoral ministers often find themselves on the same road again and again in the throes of confusion, malaise, despair, and loss of idealism. Parish life can cause pastoral ministers to feel like they're on a treadmill, challenging them continually to search for the energy needed to do their ministry, often resulting in burnout. Yet, it is only when we are "on the road" that we encounter the risen Christ who transforms our lives, heals our pain, and renews our energy and vision. The Emmaus story provides pastoral ministers with a template for ministry while at the same time providing a vehicle for personal and ministerial renewal, inspiring each of us to get back on the same road, but in a new or renewed direction.

> *Now that very day two of them were going to a village seven miles from Jerusalem called Emmaus, and they were conversing about all the things that had occurred. And it happened that while they were conversing and debating, Jesus himself drew near and walked with them, but their eyes were prevented from recognizing him. He asked them, "What are you discussing as you walk along?" They stopped, looking downcast. One of them, named Cleopas, said to him in reply, "Are you the only visitor to Jerusalem who does not know of the things that have taken place there in these days?" And he replied to them, "What sort of things?" They said to him, "The things that happened to Jesus the Nazarene, who was a prophet mighty in deed and word before God and all the people, how our chief priests and rulers both handed him over to a sentence of death and crucified him. But we were hoping that he would be the one to redeem Israel; and besides all this, it is now the third day since this took place. Some women from our group, however, have astounded us: they were at the tomb early in the*

morning and did not find his body; they came back and reported that they had indeed seen a vision of angels who announced that he was alive. Then some of those with us went to the tomb and found things just as the women had described, but him they did not see." And he said to them, "Oh, how foolish you are! How slow of heart to believe all that the prophets spoke! Was it not necessary that the Messiah should suffer these things and enter into his glory?" Then beginning with Moses and all the prophets, he interpreted to them what referred to him in all the scriptures. As they approached the village to which they were going, he gave the impression that he was going on farther. But they urged him, "Stay with us, for it is nearly evening and the day is almost over." So he went in to stay with them. And it happened that, while he was with them at table, he took bread, said the blessing, broke it and gave it to them. With that their eyes were opened and they recognized him, but he vanished from their sight. Then they said to each other, "Were not our hearts burning within us while he spoke to us on the way and opened the scriptures to us?" So they set out at once and returned to Jerusalem where they found gathered together the eleven and those with them who were saying, "The Lord has truly been raised and has appeared to Simon!" Then the two recounted what had taken place on the way and how he was made known to them in the breaking of the bread.

—Luke 24:13-35

1
Losing Our Sense of Direction
"Going to a Village Named Emmaus"

*Now that very day two of them were going to a village
seven miles from Jerusalem called Emmaus. . . .*
—Luke 24:13

Why *Not* Go to Emmaus?

Going to Emmaus probably sounded like a good idea at the
time. Jerusalem was filled with bad memories; memories of pain,
defeat, humiliation, and death. Going anywhere sounded better
than staying in Jerusalem. Why not go to Emmaus? Maybe in
Emmaus things would be better. Maybe in Emmaus, the pain
would subside, the memories would fade, and in general, things
would be different. There was only one problem: THERE WAS
NOTHING IN EMMAUS!

The two disciples who set out for Emmaus on that first Easter
Sunday in this wonderful story found in the twenty-fourth chapter of Luke's gospel had lost their sense of direction. Why
Emmaus? *Where* is Emmaus? Even today, scripture scholars and
historians dispute the location of the village named Emmaus. The
fact is the two disciples weren't so much trying to get *to* Emmaus
as they were trying to get *away from* Jerusalem. The opening line
of this story reveals to us that the two main characters are running
away from something. A village seven miles *from* Jerusalem sounded like a good, satisfying place to be after all the disciples had been
through. At this point, Jerusalem was just too much for them to
handle.

Jerusalem was the focal point of the Jewish faith, a faith that
had taken on new meaning with Jesus. Jerusalem was also the location where Jesus made his triumphal entry on Palm Sunday just a
few days earlier. It was the place where Jesus' ministry reached its

climax: where he ate and drank with his apostles at the Last Supper, where he was betrayed, arrested, denied, abandoned, scourged, crowned with thorns, made to carry a wooden cross, crucified, and buried. For these two disciples, Jerusalem was a place to get away from—as far as possible. Why *not* go to Emmaus? The gospel of Luke tells us that Emmaus was seven miles from Jerusalem. In scripture, the number seven tends to be a good number, representing fullness, completeness or perfection. Creation took seven days. Revelation tells us that the seventh trumpet will signal the end of time. The walls of Jericho fell after seven days of trumpet blasting. Don't forget how many times Jesus told Peter to forgive his brother. Peter thought seven times would be about right. Jesus responds with "not seven times but *seventy-seven* times!" To the disciples on the road leading away from Jerusalem, seven miles seemed a good, safe distance from the pain they had experienced there.

A Safe Distance From Jerusalem

We are fortunate to have the story of these two disciples on the road to Emmaus. As ministers in the Lord's church, we, too, are on a journey. The amazing encounter that unfolds on this dusty road provides each of us with an inspirational framework for renewal in our ministry. Like these two disciples, we often experience pain and loss in our lives and in our ministry. We all have our Jerusalems; those places where we once walked with the Lord but now associate with losing him. We all have our Emmauses too; those places we run to in order to put a safe distance between ourselves and the pain we have encountered. When we experience pain in our ministry, our first response is usually to get as far away from the pain as possible. We learn this as children: when our hand gets too close to the fire, we scream "ouch!" and run in the other direction. We usually have no idea where we are running to, but we are very sure of what we are running *away from!*

Wouldn't it be wonderful if our ministry never involved any pain or suffering? Unfortunately, that is wishful thinking. Pain and suffering are as much a part of ministry as they are a part of life. They come in all different shapes and sizes, including the following:

- Your Pastoral Associate position in the parish is eliminated.
- The new DRE tells you that your services as a catechist are no longer needed.
- The mentor you always relied on retires, moves away, or worse yet, dies.
- You experience a loss or tragedy in your personal life that makes it difficult to minister.
- The RCIA ministry you worked so hard at "fails" or falls far short of expectations.
- The pastor and you are not getting along.
- A re-structuring of ministry in the parish leaves your role as associate pastor depleted.
- Funding for your social ministry is drastically cut.
- Coworkers and support staff are let go, leaving you virtually alone to do the ministry.
- Ideological differences with the church leave you feeling like you don't belong.
- You just can't get through to your students.
- A child you've been reaching out to pulls further away.
- The faculty you are entrusted to lead as principal turns against you.
- You encounter conflict at every turn.
- You are constantly being criticized from both sides.

Whatever your position may be, ministry involves pain. Following Jesus involves pain. In baptism, we made a commitment to follow Jesus—and the road he takes us on leads to Jerusalem, the capitol of pain. The key is how we react to the pain we encounter in ministry. We can try to run away from the pain. However, the Emmaus story teaches us that when we walk the road with Jesus, our pain is transformed. The Emmaus story teaches us to embrace pain and suffering, acknowledge it, enter into it, and deal with it so that we may be healed. Emmaus may sound like a good safe place to go, but remember, the only thing we'll find there is the pain we tucked away in our traveling bags . . . the pain we thought we were running away from!

My Own Road to Emmaus

For myself, I encountered the road to Emmaus in the 1989-90 school year. I was in my ninth year of teaching high school religion at an archdiocesan Catholic high school in Chicago. It was a place where I encountered the Lord, walked with him, ate and drank with him, listened to him and taught his words. Over the years, I had worked my way up the ladder of Catholic employee success, finally getting my salary, which had started at $11,000, to over $20,000! On that salary, I got married, began raising a family of two children, and completed a Master's Degree at Loyola University. I had also gained the titles of Department Chair, Director of Liturgy, and Director of Public Relations. In January of 1990, however, everything came crumbling down. Without any advance warning, planning, or consultation, the archdiocese announced that it was closing the school at the end of that school year.

Students, parents, alumni, and faculty were shocked. Parents and students came to me with tears in their eyes asking, "How can they do this?" For myself, after struggling financially for nine years and dedicating my best efforts to my ministry, my reaction was "That's the thanks I get?" This question quickly gave way to the more sobering query of "Where will the next paycheck come from?" The experience was quite painful and convinced me at the time that as far as employment went, I needed to get as far away from the church as I could. *Anywhere* and *anything* would do as long as I was far away from the pain and hurt. I set out on the road to Emmaus.

For me, Emmaus turned out to be a company named Phar-Mor, a national chain of discount pharmacies. Since I had an upbringing in a family pharmacy, it seemed like the logical choice to make. It made no difference to me where I was going *to* as long as it was away *from* where I had spent the last nine years. Before I could make up my mind, however, I met the risen Lord on the road to Phar-Mor.

During one of the last months before the school closed, I was scheduled to speak at a local parish on the topic of spirituality. Although my spirits were down in the dumps, I mustered up enough strength to go out and do the presentation. My wife waited up for me knowing that I would probably come home exhausted and burned out because of everything that we were going through. She couldn't believe her eyes when at 10:30 p.m. that night I came barreling through the door with energy, enthusiasm, and excitement. She asked me what happened and I told her that I had an experience that evening that I knew I would never get working for Phar-Mor. I felt so filled with the Holy Spirit after engaging a lively audience in a wonderful evening of sharing about our faith and spirituality—something that often happened to me when teaching my high school students.

Time and again, I had encountered the Lord in the faithful that I was called to serve. In my ministry, the Spirit would often take over and guide the proceedings in directions I could never have dreamed of. I told my wife that I couldn't walk away from something that God had clearly called me to. Somehow, the Lord would make it work. I said "No" to Phar-Mor, turned around, and headed right back to church work as a Pastoral Associate and Director of Religious Education at a wonderful parish where I spent the next seven years. During that time, I prayed that the Lord would heal the pain that had occurred as a result of that school closing. Through the power of the Holy Spirit, that pain has been transformed and here I am over a decade later still ministering in the church.

By the way, Phar-Mor went bankrupt a few years later.

Losing Our Sense of Direction

The story above has a happy ending, as does the Emmaus story. However, the bottom line is that I experienced pain and, for a time, lost my sense of direction. This is a common experience for those of us who minister in the church. If you feel that you have lost your sense of direction in your ministry, you are not alone. In fact, you're in very good company. Look at all the great characters from scripture who lost their sense of direction at one time or another:

• Abram and Sarai had no idea where Canaan was . . . God had to show them.

- Jacob's son Joseph was lost in a cistern and then in a strange land called Egypt.
- The people of Israel were lost in the slavery of Egypt.
- Moses and the people of Israel were lost for forty years in the desert.
- Jonah was lost in the belly of a large fish.
- The people of Israel were lost in exile in Babylon.
- Jeremiah was lost in a dungeon and a cistern.
- Jesus was lost in the Temple at age twelve.
- The disciples were lost at sea during a storm.
- The Prodigal Son was lost to his father.
- A certain sheep in a flock of 100 was lost.
- Paul was lost in a shipwreck at sea.

Not to mention the two disciples heading off for Emmaus. They were lost too. Through the grace of God, all of these people found their way . . . and so will we.

I Once Was Lost . . .

Knowing that others have been lost before you may be a small consolation—misery *does* love company. However, this is where the good news of Jesus comes in. Jesus himself said, "The Son of Man has come to seek and to save what was lost" (Lk 19:10). If you *are* lost, REJOICE! Being lost is a prerequisite to being found! In fact, if anything was upsetting to Jesus, it was encountering people who felt that they did not need assistance in finding their way to salvation. Jesus called these people "self-righteous" and warned them that the tax collectors and prostitutes (those who were lost) would enter the kingdom of God before them (Mt 21:31). The Pharisees were among this group.

Of course, Jesus did not mean that it was preferable to be a tax collector or a prostitute. What is preferable is to own up to failures and to realize when you have strayed. Jesus said that "those who are healthy do not need a physician; but the sick do. I have not come to call the righteous to repentance, but sinners" (Lk 5:31). It is the marginalized who in Jesus' eyes are blessed because they know they are lost. The Beatitudes (Mt 5:3-12) paint a beautiful portrait of what it means to be blessed. The blessing is not in being poor, sorrowing, or hungry. The blessing is that those who are poor, sorrowing and hungry know they need to be found. Not only are they blessed, but they should "Rejoice and be glad!" (Mt 5:12).

Unfortunately, when we are lost, we often become like the Pharisees, refusing to admit that we cannot find our own way. Like the stubborn husband driving the family car in circles and refusing his wife's suggestion to pull over and look at a map, we sometimes refuse to admit that we are hopelessly lost. Jesus is The Way, but we cannot follow him if we think we can find the destination ourselves. When we come to the realization that we are lost, we are on the threshold of conversion . . . a change of direction. Being lost is a spirit-filled moment. In fact, scripture tells us that the Spirit *led* Jesus out into the wilderness, a place where getting lost is deadly. It was there that he was tempted (another word for losing one's sense of direction) and instead discovered that following not his own will but the will of his Father was the way to salvation. It was this realization that would lead Jesus to tell those who wished to follow him that "whoever wishes to save his life will *lose* it, but whoever *loses* his life for my sake and that of the gospel will save it," (Mk 8:35). Not only is it okay for us to be lost . . . it is a *requirement!*

But Now I Am Found

Jesus did not just accidentally happen upon the two disciples on the road to Emmaus. As the Good Shepherd, Jesus constantly patrols the road to Emmaus searching for those who have lost their sense of direction. In the parable of the Lost Sheep (Mt 18:10-14), Jesus teaches that a man who loses one sheep out of a hundred will go in search of the lost one. "And if he finds it, amen, I say to you, he rejoices more over it than over the ninety-nine that did not stray. In just the same way, it is not the will of your heavenly Father that one of these little ones be lost."

So when we find ourselves drifting and feeling alone on the road to Emmaus, we can take heart: Jesus is waiting for us just around the bend to show us the way.

When we were lost and could not find the way to
you, you loved us more than ever.

—*The Sacramentary,*
Eucharistic Prayer for Masses of Reconciliation, I

Finding Ourselves: A Prescription for Sabbatical

Each of us has had or will have our own Emmaus experience ...
a time in our ministry when the pain becomes so severe that the
only viable solution is to move on. Before we go any further, let
me state emphatically that there is nothing wrong with moving
on! There is a difference between running away and transitioning.
Sometimes, it is the right decision to move on, to change ministries, or even leave professional ministry altogether. God may be
calling us to do just that. More often than not, however, God is
calling us to take a step back, re-evaluate, make the necessary
adjustments, and head right back into our original ministry. In
order to accomplish this, we *need* to create space between ourselves and the various painful or toxic situations in our ministry.
The disciples *needed* to be on that road. *We* need to be on that
road. It is on that road that the transformation takes place that
allows us to return to our pain, integrate it into our being, and
finally move on.

One of the ways people achieve this re-integration is by taking
a *sabbatical* or an extended break from their ministry. The very word
Sabbath means to cease from the activity that fills ordinary everyday life—activity that can often cause pain and suffering. Genesis
tells us that God created the world in six days, rested on the seventh, and then instituted this Sabbath day of rest as part of the Law.
While we all need to take a day of rest each week, sometimes we
need an extended Sabbath or sabbatical from our ministry.
Especially if we have experienced pain in it.

If you can arrange to take a sabbatical, great! Not many ministers have this luxury. For most lay ministers, a sabbatical means the
cessation of salary and benefits. The key is to somehow provide
ourselves with the refreshed outlook and renewed energy that we

get from a sabbatical even if we can't actually take one. This is something that an encounter with the risen Lord on the road to Emmaus can provide. Just how this happens is the focus of the rest of this book . . . read on!

QUESTIONS FOR REFLECTION
- Where is your "Jerusalem," that place or time in your ministry in which you experienced hurt and pain? How did you react to it?
- Describe a time when you set out on the road to Emmaus (e.g., lost your sense of direction in your ministry).
- How open are you to being led by the Spirit?
- When was a time that you refused to admit that you were lost?
- Describe a time when Jesus "found" you.

INSIGHT

If I find Him with great ease, perhaps He is not my God. If I cannot hope to find Him at all, is He my God? If I find Him wherever I wish, have I found Him? If He can find me whenever He wishes, and tells me Who He is and who I am, and if I then know that He Whom I could not find has found me: then I know He is the Lord, my God: He has touched me with the finger that made me out of nothing.

—Thomas Merton[1]

SCRIPTURE FOR PRAYER
You guide me along the right path
for the sake of your name.
Even when I walk through a dark valley,
I fear no harm for you are at my side;
your rod and staff give me courage.

—Psalm 23:3-4

2
Losing Our Sense of Vision
"Their Eyes Were Prevented From Recognizing Him"

*And it happened that while they were conversing and
debating, Jesus himself drew near and walked with
them, but their eyes were prevented from recognizing
him. . . .*

—Luke 24:15-16

How Could They Not Recognize Him?

The Emmaus story clearly indicates that the two travelers on
the road were disciples of Jesus without actually using the word
disciples. After speaking of the experience that the Apostles and the
women had at the empty tomb (Lk 24:1-12), Luke begins the
Emmaus story by referring to the two on the road as "two of
them" (Lk 24:13). The "two of them" proceed to talk quite vivid-
ly about their experience of Jesus in a manner that clearly indicates they knew him intimately. Finally, they refer to the witnesses of the empty tomb as "women from *our* group," (Lk 24:22).
Clearly these two travelers were *disciples*. A common Christian
understanding of disciples are "those who follow Jesus." That
leaves me with one simple question: HOW COULD THEY
NOT RECOGNIZE HIM?

They walked with him. They talked with him. They ate with
him. They saw him perform miracles. They heard him preach.
They saw him put to death only three days before. Now, as they
were mourning his death, he comes to walk alongside of them and
they don't know him from Adam!

Pardon me for speaking so bluntly, but my first reaction to this
story has always been "These two must be a couple of yahoos! If

I had been there, *I* would have recognized Jesus! *I* would have gotten on my knees right then and there. No way I would not have recognized Jesus!

The truth is, most of us react to the story the way I just described. From our safe distance, it is easy to say that these travelers were clearly foolish and that we would have done better. Actually, throughout the gospels, we tend to react that way. *We* wouldn't have denied Jesus like Peter. *We* wouldn't have betrayed him like Judas. *We* wouldn't have fled like the other apostles. *We* wouldn't have doubted like Thomas. And *we* certainly wouldn't have been so blind as to not recognize Jesus on the road to Emmaus just three days after we saw him put to death.

This is easy to say from our vantage point. However, scripture has a way of inviting us to enter into the stories where we realize that perhaps we are not at all different from the many faulty characters that called themselves followers of Jesus. In fact, if we believe that the scriptures are truly *our* story, then we need to read the stories as though they are about us—as though *we* are the main characters in the stories interacting with Jesus.

The Emmaus story is no exception. In fact, the Emmaus story makes it even easier for us to enter into the story by employing a clever literary device. It seems that the author tells us the name of only one of the two disciples (Cleopas in Luke 24:18) The other disciple remains nameless. Who is this mystery character? Why is he not named? (In fact, we are not even sure if he is a "he." The story never explicitly identifies this other disciple as a man.) All we know is that this person is a follower of Jesus who is lost both in direction and in the ability to recognize the Lord. Sounds like it could be anyone! It could be you. It could be me!

Perhaps the author of the story left the name of this disciple out so that the reader could more easily enter into the story, identify with the character, and realize that we too are unable to recognize Jesus at times. The truth is, the other disciple *is* you and me! *We* are followers of Jesus who somehow lose the ability to recognize him walking right alongside of us on the road of our lives. How is it that *we* do not recognize Jesus in our daily lives, in those we work with, and in those we serve? The question, then, is not "How could *they* not recognize him?" but instead, "How could *we* not recognize him?"

"I Can't See! I Can't See!"

I must confess to being a *Three Stooges* fan. Of course, if you're a *Stooges* fan, you know that the best episodes are with Curly. One scene that Curly was famous for was when he cried out to Moe and Larry in a panic, "I can't see! I can't see!" Moe and Larry run to his aid and ask, "What's wrong?" to which Curly replies, "I've got my eyes closed!"

The truth is, "blindness" need not be a physical condition of the cornea or retina in order for one to suffer its effects. We often suffer from blindness even though our eyes are fully functional. The two disciples on the road could see clearly. Yet, they were blind. In our own ministry, we too suffer from blindness. Somehow, like the two on the road to Emmaus, we seem to be unable to recognize the Jesus who is walking right next to us. All we see is pain, frustration, hurt, and negativity. All we see is that which is wrong and in need of repair. With so much blocking our vision, it is no wonder that sometimes *we* lose our ability to see the risen Lord in our midst.

Disciples of Jesus who do not recognize him in their midst are unable to effectively minister to others. They are only able to wander off to Emmaus dwelling on the pain. In fact, if we are unable to recognize Jesus in our midst, we have no right to minister at all. Yet, many of us lose sight of the Lord in our ministry. Like the two disciples on the road, we often find ourselves consumed by negativity, drained of our sense of mission, and quite blind. We long to once again recognize Jesus alive in our ministry. We long for the days when we used to be able to reach out and touch Jesus. Now, he seems so far away. In fact, it seems as though he is gone and we are alone.

The truth is, however, that he never left. He is still walking alongside us. The problem is, our eyes are closed.

Looking for Clues

From time to time in my travels to parishes to give presentations, I lose my ability to recognize which direction I am going.
One summer, I did eight presentations for eight different parishes
in ten evenings for *Theology on Tap*, a fine catechetical program for
young adults in the Archdiocese of Chicago. With a bevy of maps
at my side, I set out each night to find my next destination. By the
final night, my head was spinning from all the activity. After the
presentation at a parish about an hour from home, I was convinced that a right turn out of the parish driveway onto the main
road would start me on the way back to my neighborhood. For
the next fifteen or twenty minutes, even though I soon began
noticing buildings and landscape that I couldn't recall seeing on
my way to the parish, I just kept driving. It took me a half-hour
to finally admit I was heading the wrong direction and was lost.
The clues were there all along. I just needed to pay attention to
them.

The same is true of our ministry. We may be heading down a
road thinking we are on course, even though we have lost sight of
Jesus somewhere along the way. We find ourselves feeling very
much alone in those times. We seem to be unable to find Jesus
anywhere. And yet, we keep heading full-steam-ahead toward our
Emmaus—that place where we find nothing! We are like Moses
leading the Israelites through the desert, desperately in need of a
recognizable landmark that will point the way to the Promised
Land.

All of us need clues to help us realize just how blind and lost
we've become in our ministry. Here are some clues or "symptoms"
that indicate that we have lost our sense of vision in ministry:

- You can detect a noticeable contrast (deterioration) to
  the previous quality/quantity of your work.
- You are experiencing chronic fatigue.
- Irritability has become a trademark of your personality.
- You find yourself radically over-extended . . . you are no
  longer "on top" of things.
- You feel guilty about your performance.
- Your recreation is becoming joyless.

- Physical symptoms are becoming manifested (more colds that last longer, weight gain or loss, etc.).
- You are experiencing lost idealism coupled with increased cynicism.
- You find yourself falling into a mechanical approach to your ministry rather than a personal approach.
- You react with anticipatory revulsion at the prospect of contact with people.
- You are experiencing a diminished capacity for beauty.
- You seem to have lost the ability to care.

This checklist is not scientific. It is more like putting your hand on a forehead to detect a fever. However, these items may give you an indication of whether or not you have lost your sense of vision in your ministry. When this happens, we call it *burnout*. Before we go any further, however, it is important to note that there is a prerequisite to claiming burnout: you need to have previously been "on fire." The two disciples who had lost their sense of direction had previously been on fire by the message of Jesus and had a good sense of direction for their ministry. Now, all that was gone. Running to Emmaus was *not* their usual choice of destination. Unless we have previously been on fire and on target with our ministry, we cannot claim burnout. Those who do are only chronic complainers who like the safety of Emmaus and want to cast aspersions from a safe distance.

Often, our experiences that lead to loss of vision and burnout are less dramatic than the one that the disciples encountered with the death of Jesus. The "deaths" that we experience in our ministry are often subtle, slow deaths—more like erosions. Little by little, we find ourselves losing our sense of vision until we are not sure just where it is we are heading and where Jesus is in our lives. For most of us, burnout occurs gradually. However, all it takes is one dramatic or significant experience to push us over the edge and put us on the road to nowhere.

Jesus, Where Are You?

Many people have a copy of a very popular reflection entitled "Footprints" in which a person looks back over the sands of time and sees only one set of footprints during the most difficult times. The bewildered individual confronts God asking the Lord why he or she was left alone during these critical times. God replies, "My child, it was during those difficult times that I carried you." This reflection can be seen in so many places that it has almost become cliché. Yet, it seems to have touched a nerve with people, the same nerve that the Emmaus story hits. When times are difficult, Jesus often seems to be missing or out of reach.

Emmaus is not the first time that troubled disciples seemed to be unable to access their Lord. The gospel story of the calming of the storm (Mt 8:23-27, Mk 4:35-41, Lk 8:22-25) tells us that Jesus and his disciples got into the boat to cross to the other side of the lake. (The invitation to get into the boat comes from Jesus: he invites the disciples to navigate the waters despite the danger of storms. It is also interesting to note that the other side of the lake was Gentile territory, indicating a whole new venue for the ministry of Jesus and his disciples, something the disciples were apprehensive about.) When a storm erupts the disciples fear for their lives. They look for Jesus but he is asleep in the stern. Just like the disciples on the road to Emmaus, they feel very much abandoned in the midst of great fear.

Luckily, they awaken Jesus and he calms the storm, leading them to ask, "Who then is this, who commands even the winds and the sea and they obey him?" (Lk 8:25). It is only after reaching Gentile territory when Jesus feeds the thousands that Peter is able to come to the conclusion that Jesus is the Messiah of God. Like the Emmaus story, it is only through the breaking of bread that eyes are opened.

In our own lives, we often feel alone at the most troubling of times. Jesus seems to be out of reach or unrecognizable during our own periods of storminess. We need to hear Jesus' words to the disciples, "Where is your faith?" (Lk 8:25) and believe that he will calm the storms of *our* lives, for faith is nothing more than trusting in the God that we cannot see. We need to recognize and trust that Jesus is present with us in the boat, on the road, and through the sands of time. When we trust, only then will our eyes be opened.

You're Not the First to Lose Sight of Jesus

Losing sight of Jesus is a frightening experience. At the same time, it is a common experience. Jesus' own parents lost sight of him. The story of the finding in the Temple (Lk 2:41-52) presents us with a foreshadowing of what it is like to travel with Jesus to Jerusalem. I used to wonder what the point was of this story. Was it a story to teach us how a young Jesus came to grips with his divinity? Or was it only a story intended to fill in the cracks concerning Jesus' hidden life as a child. I realize now that this story is like a prelude or overture to the entire gospel, capturing in a "nutshell" what the total experience of discipleship involves.

In Jerusalem, at age twelve, Jesus is lost to his parents for three days. Years later, after his crucifixion and death, he will be lost again for three days. The gospel tells us that after the Passover feast, on their way home, Mary and Joseph "journeyed for a day and looked for him among their relatives and acquaintances, but *not finding him*, they returned to Jerusalem to look for him" (Lk 2:44-45). Mary's comment "Your father and I have been looking for you with great anxiety" (Lk 2:48) seems to summarize what happens to *us* when *we* follow Jesus to Jerusalem and lose sight of him: our anxiety increases. Mary and Joseph (unlike the two disciples on the road to Emmaus) realize that they will find Jesus in the same place they lost him: Jerusalem! We, too, will find Jesus alive in the same place where he was lost to us in death: our own individual "Jerusalems"—those places of pain, frustration, and even death to which we must return.

Lord, When Did We See You?

When all is said and done, the only thing that matters in this life is whether or not we have found the Lord. In Matthew 25, when Jesus speaks about the final judgment, he doesn't tell us that we will be judged on whether or not we kept certain laws or rules or gave so much money to charity or attended certain holy days of obligation. The only criteria Jesus presents for our final judgment is whether or not we have *recognized* him in the least of our brothers and sisters. We need to be careful that we are not like the unrighteous who say to Jesus, "Lord, when did we *see* you hungry or thirsty or a stranger or naked or ill or in prison and not minister to your needs?" (Mt 25:44). Jesus tells us that we must recognize his presence in everyone we meet for "whatever you did for one of these least brothers of mine, you did for me" (Mt 25:40). We may indeed lose sight of Jesus from time to time in our ministry. Like the disciples on the road to Emmaus, however, we *can* come to recognize him once again in our midst and be healed.

> *God inspired speech in different tongues*
> *to proclaim one faith.*
> *May he strengthen your faith*
> *and fulfill your hope of seeing him face to face.*

> —*The Sacramentary,*
> Solemn Blessing #9, Holy Spirit

QUESTIONS FOR REFLECTION

- When was a time in your ministry when it seemed like you were alone and Jesus was nowhere to be found?
- How aware are you of the Lord's presence in your ministry? What are the signs of his presence?
- What symptoms or clues of "burnout" have you experienced?
- How clear is your vision for ministry?
- What ministerial setting challenges you the most right now?
- In whom do you have difficulty recognizing Jesus' presence?
- What role does *trust* play in your ministry? In your personal life? In your prayer life?

INSIGHT

We need the eyes of deep faith to see Christ in the broken body and dirty clothes under which the most beautiful One among the sons of men hides. It is seeing *that made Father Damien the apostle of the lepers, that made St. Vincent de Paul the father of the poor.*

—Mother Teresa[2]

SCRIPTURE FOR PRAYER

> *How long, Lord? Will you utterly forget me?*
> *How long will you hide your face from me?*
> *How long must I carry sorrow in my soul,*
> *grief in my heart day after day?*
> *How long will my enemy triumph over me?*
>
> *Look upon me, answer me, Lord, my God!*
> *Give light to my eyes lest I sleep in death.*

—Psalm 13:1-4

3
Talking in Circles and the Gift of Empathy
"What Are You Discussing?"

He asked them, "What are you discussing as you walk along?"

—Luke 24:17

Walking (and Talking) in Circles

I've never seen a map of the road from Jerusalem to Emmaus, but I can guess it might look something like this:

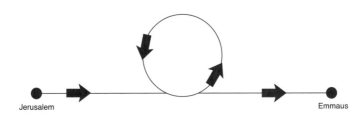

In other words, at some point on the road to Emmaus, one runs the risk of walking in circles!

The two disciples on the road found themselves going in circles—in other words, they were getting nowhere. As Jesus approached and asked them what they were discussing as they walked along, it turned out that they were re-hashing the experience of Calvary, trying to make some sense out of it. Who can blame them? The only problem is, they were so caught up in their pain, they were unable to know exactly where they were going or who it was that was walking with them. They could only see where they had just been.

It's a frustrating feeling to think that you are making progress only to find that you are going over the same piece of terrain over and over again. The truth is, in our lives and in our ministry, we find ourselves in the same predicament: repeatedly talking about the painful experiences of our past, and all the while, unable to make any forward progress on our journey.

Hello? Remember Me?

Several years ago, when I was taking a course in spirituality, the professor asked us to begin each class with some faith-sharing based on assigned scripture passages. She gave one rule: no discussion. We were only to listen to the others as they shared their reflections on scripture and its impact on their spiritual life. We were given fifteen minutes for three of us to share. On the first day in our small group, one of the participants shared what had been a somewhat frustrating and painful experience from her previous ministerial position. She took twelve of the fifteen minutes leaving the other two of us only 90 seconds each to share a thought or two! Since we were instructed not to discuss or respond, we simply bit our tongue and practiced empathy.

The second day, we got into our same groups to begin sharing. No sooner did we sit down to begin sharing than the same participant shared the exact same story she had told us the day before. I wanted to shout, "*HELLO? REMEMBER ME? YOU TOLD US THIS STORY YESTERDAY!*" Once again, however, because of our instructions, we were unable to interrupt or discuss, so we took a deep breath and practiced even more empathy.

During the break, I found my other partner and commented that it was unbelievable what we were going through. Her reply, however, caught me by surprise. Instead of chiming in on my criticism, she said, "She must be stuck in the same place and can't move on." I compare this to the disciples on the road to Emmaus and realize that this is what happens when we experience pain: we are unable to move on, unable to even notice others because all we can feel is our own hurt. When this happens to us, we find ourselves going in circles, unable to see clearly where we are headed and who is walking along with us.

"But It Feels Good to Curse the Darkness!"

Often in our ministry, we get stuck in the same place. Working in ministry can wear us down. Our ideas and suggestions can get roughed up and trampled by others until we wonder why we try at all. Our coworkers, colleagues, superiors, and subordinates can sometimes let us down or seemingly even turn against us. Someone might "appoint" himself or herself as the official "naysayer" of everything we propose, thus draining our sense of enthusiasm and energy. Our ministry may not be receiving the type of support (both financial and verbal) that we had hoped for. The congregation we serve may be resistant to change of any kind. In situations like these (and in many others) we may find it more and more difficult to keep up a positive outlook. So, we fall into the alternative: *negativity*.

Instead of lighting candles, we find ourselves continually cursing the darkness. Instead of proclaiming the good news of Jesus Christ, we become heralds or "spin doctors" of negativity and cynicism, proclaiming bad news instead of good. We focus on all that is wrong with life. We even pat ourselves on the back for cursing the darkness so insightfully and effectively. The truth is, when we are down, it feels good to curse the darkness. The only problem is, when we do this, we get nowhere fast, and take others with us. We end up walking in circles.

Mea Culpa

Before we go any further, allow me to beg forgiveness for the all-too-often times I have done this myself. After twenty years in ministry, I have experienced my share of frustration and pain and have no doubt dragged down the spirits of many a coworker with my own diatribes during discussions at the coffee machine. Negativity and cynicism are truly a temptation—they look and feel quite attractive, but are truly quite harmful. It really is much better to live by the old maxim, "If you haven't got anything good to say, don't say anything at all."

The fact is, society teaches us to speak in negative terms because it is much easier to do so. The problem is, we can lull ourselves into paralysis by passing off our creative negativity as enlightened thinking. We may convince ourselves that we are the voice of the prophet when in reality we are more a doomsayer of gloom.

A good example of this was a former coworker of mine who made a habit of going about from one staff member to another, interrupting their work to talk about all of the problems with the church, big and small—from the hierarchy all the way to our colleagues in ministry. The same stories would come up again over lunch and in meetings. Everything this person said was hard to argue with—it was all true. The problem was, in the meantime, nothing positive was getting done. Worse yet, this negativity became contagious. We found ourselves gradually sinking into the quicksand of cynicism, unable to see clearly where it was that we should be heading and who was walking at our side. We thought we were being quite insightful and progressive until a new staff member came to walk alongside of us and asked if we were always so negative. It was then that we realized that we were walking and talking in circles and getting nowhere.

Stop it! Just Stop it!

One of my favorite movies of all time is *Gandhi*. Throughout the movie, the non-violent Mahatma Gandhi struggles to bridge the gap and heal the wounds between Muslims and Hindus who cannot seem to find a way to live together. In one scene, a crowd of Hindus vehemently attempts to persuade Gandhi not to go to the house of a Muslim, much the way the disciples tried to persuade Jesus not to go to the house of Matthew the tax collector. After hearing one too many anti-Muslim chants, Gandhi orders his driver to stop the car. He forcefully commands the crowds to, "STOP IT. JUST STOP IT!"

Gandhi's words of wisdom apply to all of us who, because of our pain and frustration, are stuck in the rut of negative rhetoric. It is easy for all of us to fall into the same pattern of negativity and cynicism. All of us need to hear the words of Gandhi: "Stop it! Just stop it!" We need to get beyond pointing out all of the specks in our neighbor's eyes and instead remove the painful logs from our own. We need to stop walking in circles and begin making progress in our journeys. Only then will we be able to see clearly and recognize Jesus in our midst.

Confront It and Move On

So what are we supposed to do? Ignore our pain? Look at the world through rose-colored glasses? Enter into denial? While the Emmaus story illustrates the danger of wallowing in our pain, it also teaches us that we need to *confront* our pain in a healthy and mature manner that will allow it and us to be transformed. There is a big difference between *talking from our pain* and *sharing our pain*. Talking from our pain is a one-way street; it is a monologue, not a dialogue. It seeks to change the *other*. Sharing our pain is done in a setting where there is openness to another perspective and a willingness to allow the *self* to be transformed.

The disciples on the road do not tell their story to Jesus and then walk away from him. They share their story with him and then open themselves up to an alternative perspective, allowing themselves to be challenged (more on that later). They invite Jesus to remain with them because he offers them the gift of empathy. He listens and then seems to hold out hope for a new way of understanding their pain. Although their eyes are not yet opened, they feel their hearts burning within them. Talking from one's pain only causes heartburn for the speaker *and* the listener. Sharing one's pain sets hearts on fire with hope for transformation.

In our own ministry, we need to stop spewing forth the venom of negativity in all directions. Instead, we need to occasionally take advantage of the privacy that the road to Emmaus offers us and share our pain with someone who will truly and empathetically listen and respond to us with a new perspective. If you find yourself burdened by some lingering bitterness, pain, or frustration that is causing you to be negative or cynical, sit down with someone who can offer you the gift of empathy—someone who will truly listen to you and then open your mind to the possibility of having your perspective (and your life) transformed.

Verbal Non-Violence

In the gospel, Jesus talks about replacing revenge and the "eye for an eye, tooth for a tooth" mentality of the old covenant with the alternative of "turning the other cheek" (Mt 5:38-39). Jesus was not only speaking of those situations that are physically violent. We are quite often struck *verbally* on one cheek too. It hurts. As a way of getting back, we tend to lash out with verbal violence, engaging in negative and cynical rhetoric. Jesus does not say, "When someone strikes you on the one cheek, go and complain about it to anyone who will listen!"

Turning the other cheek means responding non-violently. It means getting on with it; not complaining about how terrible it was that part of you is hurt. Turning the other cheek is not a passive act but a pro-active one. It shows that we are brave enough, strong enough, and big enough to move forward despite the pain that we have endured. We cannot and will not change the behavior of others just by complaining about them. Others may continue assailing us with negativity and hurtful words, but we will bravely turn the other cheek and move forward. We can only focus on our own transformation. It is far better for us to provide an alternative by the way we live, act, and minister. Eventually, others will come to recognize Jesus in the complexion of our lives.

Taking a Lesson From St. Paul

St. Paul took this teaching of Jesus and elevated it to a way of life. Rather than whining and complaining about our afflictions, Paul encourages us to *boast* of them. Paul does not sit around complaining about how he has been mistreated, about how terribly he was treated in the last town he visited, or even about his state of life as a prisoner. Instead, he continually turns the other cheek, confronts his pain, and allows Jesus to transform it. Paul embraces his suffering and develops a new approach to life and ministry: "I will rather boast most gladly of my weaknesses, in order that the power of Christ may dwell with me. Therefore, I am content with weaknesses, insults, hardships, persecutions, and constraints, for the sake of Christ; for when I am weak, then I am strong" (2 Cor 12:9-10).

Paul learned that we can be noisy gongs and clanging cymbals with all of our complaining and negativity. Instead, Paul mastered the power of *Shalom*, the state of being at peace, content, and whole even in the face of suffering. Shalom means "Peace be with you." It is the word the risen Christ spoke to his disciples when he first appeared to them in the Upper Room. In the midst of their pain and suffering, Jesus brings peace, contentment and healing. Shalom is not the *absence* of conflict, pain, and frustration. It is the *peace and contentment* that comes when one reaches a level of acceptance in the midst of all that.

In our ministry, we have no doubt encountered pain and frustration. Our complaints would surely be justified. We may very well be going in circles, discussing along the way all of the negativity that has clouded our vision. The Emmaus story does not leave us mired in negativity, but calls us to a transforming experience. Our prayer should be that we, too, may discover the power of *Shalom* that will lead us to move forward in our ministry, not complaining of our afflictions, but boasting of them and of the power of God that somehow sustains us despite them.

> *Heavenly Father and God of mercy,*
> *we no longer look for Jesus among the dead,*
> *for he is alive and has become the Lord of life.*
> *From the waters of death you raise us with him*
> *and renew your gift of life within us.*
>
> *Increase in our minds and hearts*
> *the risen life we share with Christ*
> *and help us to grow as your people*
> *toward the fullness of eternal life with you.*

—*The Sacramentary,* Opening Prayer,
Second Sunday of Easter

QUESTIONS FOR REFLECTION

- What are you discussing as you walk along the path of ministry? Do you find yourself engaging in more and more negativity and cynical discussion?
- Think of those who hear you talking most often. Are you bringing them light or cursing the darkness?
- If you could draw a map of your spiritual journey, when and where have you found yourself going in circles? What helps to get you back on track?

INSIGHT

St. Francis maintained that the safest remedy against the thousand snares and wiles of the enemy is spiritual joy. For he would say, "Then the devil rejoices most when he can snatch away spiritual joy from a servant of God. He carries dust so that he can throw it into even the tiniest chinks of conscience and soil the candor of mind and purity of life. But when spiritual joy fills hearts," he said, "the serpent throws off his deadly poison in vain. The devils cannot harm the servant of Christ when they see he is filled with holy joy. When, however, the soul is wretched, desolate, and filled with sorrow, it is easily overwhelmed by its sorrow or else it turns to vain enjoyments."

—St. Francis of Assisi
as quoted by Thomas of Celano[3]

SCRIPTURE FOR PRAYER

> *Have mercy on me, God,*
> *for I am treated harshly;*
> *attackers press me all the day;*
> *My foes treat me harshly all the day;*
> *yes, many are my attackers.*
> *O Most High, when I am afraid,*
> *in you I place my trust.*
> *God, I praise your promise;*
> *in you I trust, I do not fear.*
> *What can mere flesh do to me?*

—Psalm 56:2-5

4
Regaining Our Lost Idealism
"We Were Hoping"

But we were hoping that he would be the one to redeem Israel. . . .

—Luke 24:21

Of Course They Got Their Hopes Up

The disciples had gotten their hopes up. Who can blame them? They had witnessed some great miracles and heard some spellbinding preaching from Jesus. Jesus raised a little girl and a grown man from the dead. He fed thousands from five loaves of bread and two fish. He walked on water and calmed the winds and the waves. His parables made their brains swim and their hearts burn. They saw him change water into wine and sinners into saints. They saw him drive out demons and welcome in outcasts. They heard crowds chanting "hosanna to our king!" and they basked in his glory hoping that perhaps they had gotten in on the ground floor of a fledgling kingdom. It was all going so well.

And then came Calvary.

Suddenly, it was all gone. All that remained was the hurt, some lost dreams, and a dusty road to a place named Emmaus.

Wait 'til Next Year!

I find it quite easy to talk about lost hopes and dashed idealism, for you see—I'm a Chicago Cub fan! If I had a few extra pages here, I could tell you about the numerous Cub collapses beginning with the painful memories of their calamitous 1969 collapse when I was a tender ten years of age. Each year, we Cub fans get our hopes up for a world championship, and, each year, since around the end of World War I, our hopes have been dashed.

The familiar Cub chant of "wait 'til next year!" eventually evolved into "wait 'til next century" as the 1900s came to a close with nothing but a suitcase full of dashed hopes.

Luckily, for me, the pain of watching the Cubs lose year after year is nothing compared to the real pain that people experience in their lives. On the other hand, sports *does* provide us with a metaphor for life. It hurts to see your dreams constantly eluding your grasp. Like all-too-many Cub fans, many of us in our ministry eventually tend to settle for mediocrity, afraid to get our hopes up because we know they will only be dashed. It is emotionally safer to be cynical.

Disillusionment

While the Cubs were stirring up excitement and getting peoples' hopes up in the late 1960s, our church was stirring up some excitement of its own. Vatican II was being implemented in our parishes and hopes were high for a new Pentecost. I recall the excitement of seeing the priest turn around to face us and hearing him speak in English. I recall feeling like the windows had indeed been thrown open and a breath of fresh air was renewing not only the church but also the world.

As a teenager, I got involved in the parish youth group. Together, we were going to change the world. Unfortunately, our pastor had a different idea. He wasn't too thrilled with Vatican II and did all he could to hold on to the past and stifle our enthusiasm. One by one, young people dropped off until only a small core of us remained, battle-weary and frustrated, our dreams slowly slipping away.

Throughout my ministry, as a teacher, pastoral associate/DRE, and catechetical consultant, I have gotten my hopes up many times, only to see them fizzle more often than not. There is no need for me to go on and on telling you about these experiences; you've had your fair share as well. The truth is, we all tend to get our hopes up about the impact we can make on our family, our neighborhood, our parish, our diocese, our church, and the whole world. We come to our ministry with a zealous idealism that propels us into the midst of reality where rude awakenings often occur.

Over time, we may begin to harden ourselves against the painful lessons of ministry. We boast less of our training in theology and pastoral ministry and more of our well-earned degrees from the "School of Hard Knocks." The dangerous consequence of this, however, is the loss of idealism. We may feel that we are becoming wiser, more realistic, and less naïve while all along we are, in reality, lowering our standards while becoming more and more pessimistic and cynical. Even if we are not going about spewing forth negativity, we may discover that we are not offering anything positive either. Instead, we become numb and lethargic: better to feel nothing at all than to experience any roller coasters of emotions.

Desert Wanderings and Desert Murmurings

Scripture captures this roller coaster experience of idealism and pessimism in the story of the Exodus. The people of Israel rejoiced over their newfound freedom from Egypt and gave praise to God as they began their journey to the Promised Land. Hopes were high for a bright future. Unfortunately, the Red Sea got in the way. The frustrated Israelites responded by saying to Moses, "Were there no burial places in Egypt that you had to bring us out here to die in the desert? Why did you do this to us? Why did you bring us out of Egypt? . . . Far better for us to be the slaves of the Egyptians than to die in the desert" (Ex 14:11-12).

How quickly idealism fades. Moses, however, kept the faith (another word for "never losing hope") and responded by telling the people, "Fear not! Stand your ground and you will see the victory the Lord will win for you today. . . . The Lord himself will fight for you; you have only to keep still" (Ex 14:13-14). The rest, as they say, is history.

In the face of shattered dreams, we need only to keep still and fear not. Keeping still is difficult. I like to think that the phrase "keep still" is politically correct for "shut up!" Moses is telling the people to stop their negativity and their cynicism lest they drown in it: only faith will part the waters. Surprisingly, however, the grumbling continued in the Deserts of Sin and Rephidim where the Israelites questioned the ability of Moses and Aaron to provide for them.

In reply, Moses made a startling statement when he told the people of Israel that, "Your grumbling is not against us, but against the Lord" (Ex 16:8). That's a sobering thought. When we grumble about this or that in our ministry, we need to realize that our grumbling is ultimately against the Lord! While grumbling may seem harmless, in reality, it masks the real question of, "Is the Lord in our midst or not?" (Ex 17:7) The more we occupy ourselves with grumbling, the less time and energy we have to proclaim the good news that God *is* in our midst.

Beware of Lost Idealism

Does this mean that we can never be critical or call for change and reform? Not at all. It all has to do with our attitude. Grumbling offers no hope—it simply complains about the present and nostalgically longs for the past. In our ministry, we have our share of Red Seas and Deserts of Sin and Rephidim. No doubt we entered the ministry with high hopes that we could make a significant impact. Perhaps that is still the case for you. If you continue to minister with optimism and idealism, you are blessed, as are those around you. However, even the most optimistic people have their periods of darkness; those desert experiences where we come to feel that our hopes and ideals have been put on the back burner while we deal with a less-than-hoped-for reality. Like the disciples on the road to Emmaus, we may feel that the reason we originally came to Jerusalem no longer exists. What happens when we lose this sense of idealism? How does this happen?

For some of us, it can happen as a result of a significant, painful experience. For others, it may be a cumulative effect (like waiting a lifetime to see the Cubs win a pennant). Either way, the result of lost idealism is an increase in anger, fear, resentment, apathy, and cynicism. When we lose our ideals, we often end up playing the blame game, pointing fingers at those who are responsible for doing this to us.

The two disciples on the road to Emmaus engage in this finger-pointing as they explain the reason for their dashed hopes to their new walking companion: "Our chief priests and rulers both handed him over to a sentence of death and crucified him" (Lk 24:20). Loss of idealism fosters—or festers—a sense of victimization and suggests that we are engaged in a win-lose, us vs. them scenario. We have lost something and someone has to be blamed. The danger for ourselves and for others, however, is that emotions like fear, anger, and resentment are all great motivators. We may continue forging ahead in our ministry at a high level of energy, but for all the wrong reasons.

In our church today, charismatic leaders on both sides (conservative and liberal) are playing on the fear, hurt, anger, and disillusionment of those who feel their hopes have been dashed since Vatican II. Lost idealism creates vulnerability which can be easily manipulated. Loss of idealism, which can be equated with loss of faith, should not be taken lightly. It is a cancer that, left unchecked and untreated, can poison our spirits and the lives of those around us. The good news, however, is that loss of idealism is a treatable and curable malady as long as we recognize the one in our midst who heals.

The Grieving Process

In her landmark book, *On Death and Dying*, Dr. Elisabeth Kubler-Ross provided us with a look at the various stages that terminally ill patients go through: denial, anger, bargaining, depression, and acceptance.[4] Since the release of that book, we have come to know these five stages as not just belonging to those who are dying but as part of what we call the "grieving process." Grieving takes place in our lives anytime we experience the loss of something or someone significant. This applies to our lost hopes and ideals as well.

Our loss of idealism is part of a grieving process that leads us eventually to acceptance or the transformation of our fears, hurts, and angers into new hope. The grieving process eventually leads to a reinterpretation and integration of our painful experience(s). The Old Testament provides us with numerous accounts of the people of Israel re-interpreting their collective experience after their hopes had been dashed. The collapse of Israel's kingdom, the destruction of the Temple, and the resulting exile were traumatic experiences for the people of Israel who had placed all of their hopes in their monarchy and their liturgical focal point. The experience of the two disciples on the road to Emmaus is similar: Jewish people being forced to flee from the place where they thought their hopes were to be fulfilled. The road to Emmaus is their exile.

Generations in exile mulled over their experience, looking for explanations for their terrible loss. No doubt, a great deal of grumbling took place. It was within that painful experience of exile, however, that the voice of the prophet proclaimed new hope. The prophetic voice is not one that goes about rehashing the pain and pointing fingers of blame. On the other hand, the prophetic voice confronts the reality, seeks to identify a lesson that can be learned, and holds out hope for a future.

In *The Great Themes of Scripture: Old Testament*, Richard Rohr and Joseph Martos tell us that "the prophets were all optimists. They were always optimistic because they had seen the redemptive pattern of the Lord. They saw God's love breaking through again and again, overcoming human doubt and resistance, bringing salvation and new life."[5] In our own ministry, when we find ourselves in exile from our hopes and dreams, we need to seek out the voice of the prophet who helps us confront our pain, learn some difficult lessons, and emerge with a new hope and a new set of ideals. The gospel is not about victimization but about salvation, transformation and redemption.

Why Bother?

If our hopes are to be continually dashed, resurrected, and dashed again, we may wonder, "Why bother? What's the use?" The answer comes from a line that is proclaimed whenever we renew our baptismal vows. Simply put, we do it because, "THIS IS OUR FAITH. THIS IS THE FAITH OF THE CHURCH." Our faith is the belief and trust we place in the Paschal Mystery of Jesus. This means that we have placed our lives (and our ministry) within the context of dying and rising in Christ Jesus. In other words, our lives are all about dying and rising. The beautiful ritual of the Easter Vigil, the climax of the liturgical year where we celebrate the baptism of the faithful, is completely shrouded in the imagery of death and resurrection. Just look at the following excerpts from some of the prayers of the Easter Vigil:

- On this most holy night, when our Lord Jesus Christ passed from *death to life* . . . (Opening Prayer)
- That we may be confident that we shall share in his victory over *death* . . . (Opening Prayer)
- This is the night when Jesus Christ broke the chains of *death* and *rose* triumphant from the grave. (the Exultant)
- Bless this font, that those *reborn* in it may be one with his adopted children in Christ. (Liturgy of Baptism)
- Send your Spirit of adoption on those to be *born again* in baptism. (Liturgy of Baptism)
- May all who are *buried* with Christ in the *death* of baptism *rise* also with him to *newness of life*. (Blessing of Water)
- Through the paschal mystery, we have been *buried* with Christ in baptism, so that we may *rise* with him to *new life*. (Renewal of baptismal promises)

In addition, recall that the Easter Vigil is one part of a unified experience we call the *Triduum*: a celebration of the transformation of death into life. It is no accident that the Emmaus story is read during the Easter season when the neophytes, together with the assembly of the faithful, dwell upon the mysteries of our death and resurrection in Christ Jesus. Our loss of hope and idealism is part of our grieving process through which we come to encounter and recognize the risen Christ who restores hope and gives new life. Elisabeth Kubler-Ross tells us that "If a patient stops expressing hope, it is usually a sign of imminent death."[6] As a people of faith, it is a sign of imminent death when we stop expressing hope in Christ Jesus.

Are We Creating a Monster?

It is no coincidence that since the tumult of the 1960s and the end of the so-called "age of innocence" the number of civil lawsuits has increased astronomically, the result of all those with lost hopes and ideals seeking recompense and retribution. Is it any wonder that young people today often seem to be disillusioned when all they've heard from their elders is "we *were* hoping" instead of "we *are* hoping?" Do we want our loss of idealism to be our legacy and the sole inheritance of our offspring?

In the Archdiocese of Chicago, our Office for Catechesis recently had over twenty parishes seeking a full-time, qualified Director of Religious Education. Unfortunately, only seven viable candidates were available for consideration. At meetings and gatherings of DRE's, the question often went up, "Where will our successors come from?" The more we discussed this, the more we had to ask ourselves what it is that we have been saying about the ministry ("What are you discussing along the way?"). Perhaps those around us have heard us constantly lamenting about the problems we see in the church and the loss of our dreams and ideals. Dr. Robert Ludwig tells us that "today's young adults have grown up in an increasingly polarized and often cynical church, where they've heard mostly criticism about Catholicism and little of what is positive and constructive. Catholic identity is difficult to figure out in such a conflicted situation, and what is attractive and inviting about this church is not very visible to them."[7] As ministers of the gospel, we have the responsibility to proclaim to those we minister with and to the great hopes and ideals that our Lord calls us to.

Field of Dreams

As I write this, the Cubs are in the throes of another bad streak, having lost 21 of their last 28 games. I realize that in my lifetime, I have seen the Cubbies lose nearly 4,000 games! So why am I still a Cub fan? I owe it all to two fellows by the name of Jack Brickhouse and Ernie Banks. Jack Brickhouse was the voice of the Cubs for nearly forty years, including the years of my childhood (the mid-60s) when the Cubs were especially dismal. Despite this,

Jack Brickhouse greeted the television audience with such enthusiasm and optimism that you believed deep down in your heart that the Cubs really had a chance to win each and every day. His joyful shouts of "Hey, Hey!" after each home run ignited such excitement that you felt the Cubs were on their way. Ernie Banks was the lone bright star for most of that decade, pounding out 512 career home runs. In addition to his home run hitting prowess, Ernie (affectionately known as "Mr. Cub") was also known for his exuberant smile and eternal optimism that led to his trademark saying of "Let's play TWO today!" Till this day, I am convinced that these two men are responsible for creating a sense of eternal optimism about the Cubs that has been passed from generation to generation and draws millions of fans each year to a "field of dreams" that has not seen a World Series since 1945. Do we ignite the same hope about our ministry and the gospel in those we serve? Is our ministerial setting a "field of dreams?"

> *God our Father, creator of all,*
> *today is the day of Easter joy.*
> *This is the morning on which the Lord*
> *appeared to men*
> *who had begun to lose hope*
> *and opened their eyes to what the scriptures foretold:*
> *that first he must die, and then he would rise*
> *and ascend into his Father's glorious presence.*
>
> *May the risen Lord*
> *breathe on our minds and open our eyes*
> *that we may know him in the breaking of bread,*
> *and follow him in his risen life.*

—The Sacramentary,
Easter Sunday Opening Prayer

QUESTIONS FOR REFLECTION

- What hopes and ideals of yours have you seen diminish in your ministry?
- What do you hear yourself lamenting in your discussion with others?
- What is the danger of lost idealism in your ministry?
- What lost hopes and ideals do you need to grieve for?
- What is an experience you've had in which your lost hopes have been transformed into new ideals and new life?
- How have you connected your lost hopes and ideals to the Paschal Mystery?
- What *are* you hoping for? Is your ministerial setting a "field of dreams?"

INSIGHT

In deep disappointment, I have wept over the laxity of the church. But be assured that my tears have been tears of love. There can be no deep disappointment where there is not deep love. Yes, I love the church; I love her sacred walls. How could I do otherwise? Yes, I see the church as the Body of Christ. But, oh! How we have blemished that body through social neglect and fear of being nonconformists. But even if the church does not come to the aid of justice, I have no despair about the future. I have no fear about the outcome of our struggle in Birmingham and all over the nation, because the goal of America is freedom. Let us all hope that the dark clouds of racial prejudice will soon pass away and the deep fog of misunderstanding will be lifted from our fear-drenched communities and in some not too distant tomorrow the radiant stars of love and brotherhood will shine over our great nation with all of their scintillating beauty.

—Dr. Martin Luther King, Jr.[8]

SCRIPTURE FOR PRAYER

> *My God, rescue me from the power of the wicked,*
>   *from the clutches of the violent.*
> *You are my hope, Lord:*
>   *my trust, God, from my youth.*
> *On you I depend since birth;*
>   *from my mother's womb you are my strength;*
>   *my hope in you never wavers.*

—Psalm 71:4-6

5
Gaining a New Perspective
"Oh, How Foolish You Are!"

And he said to them, "Oh, how foolish you are! How slow of heart to believe all that the prophets spoke!"

—Luke 24:25

Harsh Words

First, the two disciples spill their guts to someone they think is a stranger who has joined them on the road to Emmaus. They open their broken hearts to him and share their pain. They tell him about their lost hopes. They point the finger of blame at the Jewish officials as they continue to shake the dust of Jerusalem off of their feet. They reveal just how lost, hurt, and in despair they are.

Now it's Jesus' turn to respond.

One would think that he would respond gently, with great care and sensitivity. Surely he would tend to these two lost sheep with all of the pastoral tenderness of the Good Shepherd that he is. Instead, the first words out of his mouth are: "Oh, how foolish you are!"

Ouch! These words are harsh and seem insensitive. What's going on here? What is Jesus doing?

The Truth Hurts . . . But Sets Us Free!

At first glance, it might seem that Jesus is breaking an important rule of pastoral counseling which requires the counselor to establish *empathy* with the client. We would expect Jesus to begin by saying something like, "So, what I hear you saying is. . . ." Instead, we hear Jesus tell them they are being foolish. Rather than tiptoeing around their pain and walking gingerly on the eggshells of their shattered dreams, Jesus confronts them. To tell someone that they are foolish is to suggest that they lack good sense. Jesus does not mince words here. He tells them that something is clearly wrong with their thinking. Jesus engages in a practice known as constructive *confrontation*.

Author Gerard Egan describes confrontation as "an invitation to examine some form of behavior that seems to be self-defeating or harmful to others."[9] Jesus is not being cruel, reckless or unsympathetic here. In fact, he has already shown great empathy by listening intently and at length to the story of the two disciples. Now, it is time to challenge them to grow by helping them to see the truth. Jesus engages in a practice that has become somewhat of a lost art in pastoral ministry today: facing the truth.

Keeping the Peace at the Expense of the Truth

While I was writing this chapter, I got a call from a pastoral associate at a large suburban parish where the DRE had recently left. She went on and on complaining about what a disaster this former DRE had been and whether there was some way this person's personnel file at the diocesan office could reflect these glaring deficiencies. I replied that a copy of the performance review completed by the pastor should go in her file. After a long pause, the pastoral associate told me that the pastor never did the performance review because he didn't like to evaluate people for fear of criticizing them. He wanted to keep peace at all costs—even at the expense of the truth. Instead of peace, however, he got the pieces of a broken religious education program.

Jesus has no fear of the truth—*we* do. In fact, Jesus spoke often of the truth:

- "If you remain in my word, you will truly be my disciples, and you will know the *truth*, and *the truth will set you free*" (Jn 8:32).
- "I am the way and *the truth* and the life. No one comes to the Father except through me" (Jn 14:6).
- "For this I was born and for this I came into the world, *to testify to the truth*. Everyone who belongs to the *truth* listens to my voice" (Jn 18:37).

In these three brief passages, Jesus is telling us that: 1) truth is the key to freedom, 2) the only way to the Father is through truth, and 3) the purpose of his mission can be summed up in one word: *truth!* Why is it that we fear the very essence of Jesus' gospel? The truth may sting for a short time, but it is preferable to the long drawn out pain of distorted vision.

On that road to Emmaus, Jesus knew that the first step in helping his disciples to see clearly was to get them to face up to the truth. Only in truth would their eyes be opened so that they could recognize his presence in their midst. Jesus cuts through their self-defeating thinking and challenges them to see their pain from a whole new perspective—the perspective of truth. In our ministry, Jesus calls us to the truth, challenging us to see with a whole new set of eyes and from a new perspective.

Some Perspectives on the Word *Perspective*

Many years ago, I studied Latin in high school and, believe it or not, I *do* remember some of it. In my limited knowledge of Latin, I recall that the word *perspective* comes from two Latin words: *per* meaning "through" and *specto* meaning "to see." To have perspective means to see through the distortions and distractions that cloud our vision. To have perspective means to see something in a whole new way. The Emmaus story is a story of perspective: Jesus confronts the two disciples on the road to Emmaus—not to be cruel or insensitive—but to begin the process of opening their eyes to a truth that will set them free.

Perhaps the best way to understand perspective might be to talk about what it means to lose perspective. When we say that someone has lost their perspective, we are saying that they are incapable of seeing reality as it truly is: they are either missing something, forgetting something, not recognizing something, or blowing something way out of proportion. When we say that we need to get another perspective, we are suggesting that we should look at the same thing from someone else's vantage point because our own view is obstructed or skewed. In sports, instant replays from multiple camera angles allow us to get several different perspectives on the same play: a base runner may look *safe* from one angle but clearly *out* from another.

Perspective also relates to how sharp our focus is. In the children's television program *Rugrats*, talkative babies Tommy and Chuckie are constantly frightened by shadows and shapes in the dark that appear to them as monsters. As soon as the light goes on, they see more clearly that what they thought was a monster is really just a harmless toy or tree. How often in our own heads do we create mountains out of molehills and monsters out of moppets?

Finally, another key to understanding perspective is that it helps us define how large something is in relation to something else. Basketball great Michael Jordan may seem like a skyscraper . . . that is, until you stand him next to the Sears Tower or the Empire State Building by which he would be dwarfed. Likewise, the planet we live on seemed extraordinarily immense until Apollo 8 sent back the first photographs of the earth from the perspective of the moon. Suddenly, our earth seemed to be just another object in the night sky.

So, what does all of this talk about perspective teach us about our lives and our ministry? It teaches us that the way we are presently seeing things is not the only way to see things. In fact, our vision may be totally out of perspective. The disciples on the road to Emmaus had lost so much perspective that they couldn't even recognize Jesus a few feet away from them. Perhaps Jesus' words to the disciples on the road ("Oh, how foolish you are!") may apply to us. Perhaps we need to gain a new perspective and see with the eyes of Jesus.

Losing Perspective in Our Ministry

Often times in our ministry, we lose our perspective: our ability to see with the eyes of Christ. Like Tommy and Chuckie from the *Rugrats*, we may begin to see monsters looming at every corner waiting to eat us up. We may begin to feel that those we work with or for are out to get us. We may feel that the challenges we face are so huge that they make the prospect of feeding 5,000 people with five loaves and two fish look like a piece of cake. We may feel as though we are becoming isolated because no one understands us or our cause. We may feel as though no one appreciates or affirms our hard work. We may feel so hurt, worn out, and defeated that it seems like our efforts are not worth it. At the other extreme, we may allow our sense of self-importance to blow so out of proportion that we make ourselves out to be the center of the universe (or at least the parish). At times like this, we need what is referred to as a "Copernican revolution." Copernicus was the Polish astronomer who discovered that the earth revolves around the sun and not vice versa. His discovery of the truth changed our perspective of the whole cosmos.

Regaining Perspective

In medieval times, when monarchies were the standard form of governance, it was common practice for royalty to employ a large contingent of court officials: sages, prophets, soothsayers, and advisers to name a few. In addition to these highly respected officials, it was customary to include a *court jester* whose responsibility it was not only to provide comic relief but actually to make fun of (parody) the king and queen. Simply put, the court jester's job was to help royalty keep things in perspective. No one else was allowed to make fun of the royalty, but the court jester could do so with impunity. Richard Rohr, the well-known Franciscan author and speaker, likes to explain in his talks that the court jester's role was to remind the king that he was full of #@%★ and that we all need a court jester in our lives . . . someone who can say to us, "Oh, how foolish you are!" Each of us needs to have someone in our lives who can provide this kind of perspective— someone who can confront us with the painful truth and then stay for dinner!

Strategies for Regaining Perspective

While our perspective may be easily lost, it is also possible to regain it by taking some simple practical steps. Here are a few tips for regaining or keeping your perspective:

- *Exercise.* Spend at least thirty minutes daily engaged in some form of aerobic exercise (running, walking, etc.). A healthy body leads to a healthy mind and a healthy perspective. Personally, many major problems in my life have miraculously shrunken after a good run or walk. I run four to five miles at least three days a week and take a forty-minute walk with my wife on the days I'm not running. These moments have become precious to me and I look forward to them each day, especially when the going gets rough. The simple act of making exercise a priority is a shift in perspective. Something else must by necessity become less important in order to make room for exercise. Don't say you can't find the time—even presidents and world leaders find time to exercise regularly. If you cannot find time for thirty minutes of exercise even a few times per week, that is proof enough that something is out of whack in your perspective.

- *Humor and laughter.* Humor is another very important way for us to keep perspective in our ministry. Most of us take our ministry and ourselves far too seriously. Certainly, the gospel is serious business. At the same time, it is good news, a message of joy meant to bring fullness of life. No life can be full without the ability to laugh. At times in our ministry, we need to laugh if only to keep from crying. I personally make a habit of bringing some kind of levity into any gathering. Laughter is a form of communion, for it transcends our differences and builds community. Humor allows us to put things into perspective and see in a whole new way.

- *Self-affirmation.* In my calendar, I carry a comic strip depicting an auto mechanic diligently repairing a car engine. His grumpy boss comes up behind him and asks, "Did I tell you you're doing a good job?" The worker responds, "No," to which the boss curtly replies, "I didn't think so." This comic strip was given to me by a former employer a number of years ago—a man who treated me fairly and with respect but was, by his own admission, not the greatest at affirming people. I look at this comic strip every day to give perspective to my work. I remind myself that this day will probably pass by without anyone patting me on the back or telling me that I'm doing a good job. However, if I keep perspective and rely on an inner sense of affirmation, I can thrive in my ministry knowing deep down that I am doing the Lord's work.

- *Completing tangible tasks.* When I was a young high school teacher struggling to make ends meet, I taught five days a week and then worked on Saturdays at my uncle's pharmacy. Instead of exhausting me, however, I found that the second job helped provide perspective on my first job. Ministry involves dealing with a number of intangibles. Sowing the seeds of faith as a teacher sounds romantic but at the end of the week, one wonders whether any seed found good soil. My work in the pharmacy was completely tangible. I set up displays, unpacked orders, stocked shelves and waited on customers. I knew what my tasks were and I knew when I was done. That feeling of accomplishment is quite important and is often elusive in our ministry. Completing a tangible task, whether it be rearranging your office, putting up a bulletin board, cleaning out your files, or engaging in a hobby such as gardening or carpentry is a valuable strategy for regaining perspective.

- *Diversions.* If you live, eat, breath, dream and think about your ministry from the moment you awaken until the moment you fall asleep, you are a prime candidate for losing your perspective. Some people I know in the ministry cannot converse in any other way than "church-talk." It is absolutely crucial to your mental health to have diversions or other interests that feed and nourish you: friendships, hobbies, sports, current events, reading, music, theater, or recreation. One of my six brothers happens to be a very prominent priest in the Archdiocese of Chicago. People expect that when we get together, we talk endlessly about church business. On the contrary, after dealing with church business all week, the last thing the two of us want to do is talk shop. Instead, since we are both avid runners, we tend to engage in conversation about our latest achievements pounding the pavement. If not that, we discuss our respective allegiances to the Cubs and the White Sox (my brother, of course) or a mutual love, the Chicago Blackhawks hockey club. Throughout the year, we run in races, attend sporting events, and enjoy concerts together, often without discussing any church business at all.

- *Prayer and scripture.* Without prayer, we have no hope of maintaining perspective. It is when we pray that we see ourselves as we truly are before God. In our prayer, we gain perspective by magnifying the Lord (as Mary did) and by decreasing ourselves (as John the Baptist did). Prayer of praise is especially powerful for regaining perspective. If we just take a moment each day to reflect on how awesome God is and how God has abundantly blessed us, our problems suddenly seem to diminish. Likewise, Jesus provided the two disciples on the road with perspective by inviting them into scripture. In sacred scripture, we discover a faith-story that provides a framework for our faith life. By reading scripture daily or at least on a regular basis, we place our (singular) story within the framework of our (plural) story and gain perspective for living.

- *Look at the birds in the sky.* Literally, look at the birds! Jesus provided us with a blueprint for regaining perspective in Matthew 6:25-34 when he taught the crowds about worry and anxiety. Jesus knew that by lifting our eyes to the heavens and watching one of God's creatures soar through the vast expanse of the sky we would realize that our problems are not as big as they seemed. Jesus' famous "lilies of the field" discourse provides us with "perspective therapy." The next time you are mired in loss of perspective, lift your eyes and look for a bird soaring through the heavens and simply marvel at the majesty. When you return to your problems, they will still be there but your spirit will be lifted up and you will be capable of seeing them from a whole new perspective!

- *Talk to someone who will listen.* Perspective gets thrown out of whack when we keep things bottled up inside ourselves. The more we replay a situation over and over in our heads, the worse it becomes. The key to the Emmaus story is the fact that the two disciples share their pain with the Lord who listens and then provides a whole new perspective. Each of us needs to have some one we can turn to who will listen—someone who always seems to be able to see things differently. If we can bend their ears and borrow their eyeballs for just a few moments, it will result in a world of difference.

Frame of Reference

While I was writing this book, the plane which John F. Kennedy, Jr. was flying with his wife and sister-in-law disappeared off of Martha's Vineyard resulting in their tragic and untimely deaths. In the days that followed the tragedy, many in the flying community commented that it was dangerous to fly in the evening hours over the waters off of Martha's Vineyard because it becomes difficult to see the horizon which serves as a point of reference. Without a clear horizon, the pilot's frame of reference becomes clouded leading to confusion and danger. Like the end of a rainbow, the horizon can never be reached—it is always in the distance or transcendent. Yet, it provides us with a framework or perspective for determining our present location.

The need for a horizon also applies to our ministry. We need to have a clear and visible horizon as a frame of reference for our lives. In his "Theology of Faith" courses at Chicago's Catholic Theological Union, John Linnan refers to God as the "ultimate horizon," meaning that God is the framework or necessary back-drop for all human acts—transcendent, yet intimately related to the proximate. Everything we do or say is done or said against the background of the absolute good that is God. Losing our perspective means we have lost sight of our horizon. It means we have lost sight of the absolute good that is the backdrop or framework for all of creation.

When the Word became flesh, the ultimate horizon was made ever more visible to us. In the midst of our loss of perspective, we need to focus our eyes once again on Jesus who puts all things in perspective and helps us to see clearly, not only the ground upon which we stand, but also the direction in which we are traveling.

Jesus confronted his disciples on the road to Emmaus with the truth. This confrontation was not an attack nor was it done out of malice. When done out of love, confrontation is a sincere desire to access the truth. Gerard Egan reminds us that, "through confrontation, clients develop alternate frames of reference with regard to their experiences, behaviors, and feelings."[10] Jesus confronts each of us with the truth as we travel the road to Emmaus, providing us with an alternate frame of reference for our lives . . . a new perspective that will eventually open our eyes fully, allowing us to see the presence of God in our midst.

Almighty God and Father of light,
a child is born for us and a son is given to us.
Your eternal Word leaped down from heaven
in the silent watches of the night,
and now your world is filled with wonder
at the nearness of her God.

Open our hearts to receive his life
and increase our vision with the rising of dawn,
that our lives may be filled with his glory and his peace,
who lives and reigns for ever and ever.

—*The Sacramentary*, Christmas, Mass at Dawn,
Opening Prayer

QUESTIONS FOR REFLECTION

- What is the truth that Jesus is confronting me with at this time in my ministry? How am I presently being "foolish?"
- When was a time that I either confronted or was confronted with the truth? How did this experience lead to growth?
- When was a time I lost perspective? How might my perspective presently be out of focus?
- How does Jesus help me to see more clearly? How can Jesus be a framework (point of reference) for my ministry?
- Who in my life can confront me with the truth and still stay for dinner? Whose ears can I bend and whose eyeballs can I borrow?
- Who is my court jester, someone who makes me laugh at myself and not take myself too seriously?

INSIGHT

At the end of the Dialogue *(Catherine of Siena), God himself declares this truth: "Nothing has ever happened and nothing happens save by the plan of My divine Providence. In all things that I permit, in all things that I give you, in tribulations and in consolations, temporal or spiritual, I do nothing save for your good, so that you may be sanctified in Me and that My Truth be fulfilled in you." This is the conviction that was born . . . in the souls of the disciples of Emmaus when the Risen Christ gave them a fuller understanding of the mystery of the Cross: "O foolish," He said to them, "and slow of heart to believe in all things in which the prophets have spoken." What happened to these disciples on the way to Emmaus should happen to us too, if we are faithful, on the way to eternity. If for them and for the Apostles there had to be a second conversion, still more is such a conversion necessary for us.*

—R. Garrigou-LaGrange[11]

Scripture for Prayer

For my thoughts are not your thoughts,
nor are your ways my ways, says the Lord.
As high as the heavens are above the earth,
so high are my ways above your ways
and my thoughts above your thoughts.

—Isaiah 55:8-9

6
Renewing Our Vision
"Their Eyes Were Opened"

*And it happened that, while he was with them at
table, he took bread, said the blessing, broke it, and
gave it to them. With that their eyes were opened and
they recognized him, but he vanished from their sight.*

—Luke 24:30-31

Stay With Us

The two disciples on the road to Emmaus knew a good thing
when they saw it. This stranger walking with them was too good
to be true. They were certainly not going to let him get away. He
had listened to them with great compassion and then offered them
a challenging, exciting, fresh new perspective. After all the pain
and suffering of Calvary, they thought that they could never hope
again . . . never dream again . . . never feel good again. That is, until
this stranger came along and offered them a whole new set of eyes.

They were just beginning to feel better when the stranger
indicated that he was going to move on. Now, it looked like they
were going to find themselves alone once more. They had to find
a way to keep him. They were just beginning to see a return of the
light and now it seemed that darkness would once again enfold
them if he departed. Somehow they persuaded him to pull off of
the road with them and get a bite to eat.

This stranger, however, was not interested in being served but
in serving. The blessing, the breaking, the distributing—somehow
this bread ritual seemed familiar to the two disciples. As they took
the bread from his hands, and digested it to their stomachs, it was
their eyes that were fed. They feasted on his divine presence and
savored the sweet aftertaste of renewed clarity, vision, hopes, ideals,
and zeal. Suddenly, Emmaus didn't seem so important anymore.

Not as long as their eyes had been opened to recognize new life in the midst of their pain. In the dark of night, their eyes had awakened to a new day—and nothing would ever look the same again.

The Eyes Have It

This eye-opening experience for the two disciples from the road may have been a first for them, but it certainly wasn't the first eye-opening experience that Jesus was a part of. In fact, Jesus was so involved in restoring sight to people that one might think that he had developed an interest in optometry. A quick survey of the gospels reveals just how often Jesus was involved in either restoring or talking about sight (many of these passages are repeated throughout the synoptic gospels):

Matthew

6:22-23	"The lamp of the body is the eye . . . "
7:3-5	"Why do you notice the splinter in your brother's eye . . . "
9:27-31	"And as Jesus passed on from there, two blind men followed him . . . "
11:4-5	"Go and tell John what you hear and see: the blind regain their sight . . . "
12:22	"Then they brought to him a demoniac who was blind and mute . . . "
13:16	"But blessed are your eyes, because they see . . . "
15:29-31	"Great crowds came to him, having with them the lame, the blind . . . "
18:9	"And if your eye causes you to sin . . . "
20:30-34	"Two blind men were sitting by the roadside . . . "
21:14	"The blind and the lame approached him in the temple area . . . "
21:42	" . . . by the Lord has this been done, and it is wonderful in our eyes."
23:16	"Woe to you, blind guides . . . "

Mark

8:22-25 "When they arrived at Bethsaida, they brought to him a blind man . . . "

10:46-52 "And as he was leaving Jericho . . . Bartimaeus, a blind man . . . sat by the roadside begging."

Luke

7:21-22 " . . . he also granted sight to many who were blind."

10:23 "Blessed are the eyes that see what you see."

John

9:1-40 "As he passed by he saw a man blind from birth."

9:39 "I came into this world for judgment, so that those who do not see might see . . . "

20:29 "Blessed are those who have not seen and have believed."

Get the picture? Certainly, Jesus was moved with compassion for those who lacked physical sight. But obviously his concern went beyond physical sight. Jesus was more concerned with sight at a deeper level; something that we might call *insight*. Jesus sought to bring people to a whole new way of seeing themselves, others, and God. Jesus' teachings continue to challenge the way we normally view reality. We may not even be aware that there are alternative ways of viewing reality other than the way we presently see things. Yet, from time to time, we experience those moments or flashes of insight when we come to see things in a whole new way.

Magic Eyes

A few years ago, there was a small craze created by a line of books called *Magic Eye*. These books consist of computer-generated artwork that contain "hidden" multi-dimensional images that "pop out" of the page. The reader is directed to hold the image close to their nose so that it appears blurry but relaxes the eye and then slowly pull it away thus allowing the brain to interpret the depth of the 3-D image until the image "pops out" with perfect clarity. If you stare at the image in a normal fashion, the 3-D image remains hidden even though it is right under your nose.

At the height of this craze, crowds of people with books held to their noses gathered around the *Magic Eye* carts in the mall. Every so often, someone could be heard excitedly exclaiming, "Oh! Now I see it!" Their excitement immediately led them to invite others to share the experience.

The *Magic Eye* books prove that it is possible to have our vision transformed. This is also true about our vision for life and for our ministry. Like the disciples on the road, we may think that we are seeing things quite clearly while all along, our eyes are blinded to the presence of God right under our noses. Jesus challenges us to view reality in a radically different manner that leads us to recognize the presence of the divine in our midst. These moments of insight are called *conversion* experiences. Conversion is not a matter of changing from one denomination to another, but of changing the way we perceive reality; a life-long process! In our own ministry, we are being called to ongoing conversion; challenged to see as Jesus sees. If we, as Christ's ministers, can tend to our own conversion, we will be better equipped to facilitate the conversions of those we serve.

Repent! Let Go!

It should come as no surprise to anyone who's read the gospels that Jesus is interested in conversion. In fact, the gospel of Mark tells us that the very first words of Jesus' public ministry were: "This is the time of fulfillment. The kingdom of God is at hand. *Repent*, and believe in the gospel" (Mk 1:15). This "sound byte" from Mark captures the urgency and centrality of Jesus' message more efficiently than any contemporary public relations expert could. The word *repent* that Jesus uses here comes from the Greek word *metanoia* meaning "to change one's mind, attitude, or decision."[12] *Metanoia* suggests that we need to "turn back on the road (we) have been traveling."

After this startling call to make a U-turn on the road of life, Jesus then proceeds to lay out a new road map, his vision that challenges us to see in a whole new way. The key to adapting this new vision, however, is to *let go* of the old way of seeing things. Unfortunately, letting go does not come easy. The following story illustrates in a humorous way just how difficult it is to let go:

> One afternoon, a man named Harry went mountain climbing. All in all, things were going pretty well. Then suddenly, the path he was walking on gave way, taking Harry with it. With arms flailing, Harry managed to grab a small branch on the side of the mountain. Holding on for dear life, he screamed, "Help! Help! Is anybody up there?" Miraculously, the clouds parted and a beam of light illuminated Harry as he hung tenuously from the branch. A voice—clearly the voice of God—spoke directly to Harry and said, "Harry, I will save you. I am all that is good, all that is true, and all that has meaning. Let go, Harry; I will save you. Let go." Harry thought long and hard about this. Then with a sudden burst of conviction, he looked up the mountain and shouted, "IS ANYBODY *ELSE* UP THERE?"[13]

Letting go is easier said then done. Letting go fills us with anxiety because, like a trapeze artist flying through the air, we are never quite sure if our partner will be there at the right time and place to grab on to us before we fall. On the other hand, the exhilaration that comes from letting go of the old and grabbing on to the new is life-giving. In fact, letting go is a prerequisite to learning any new skill.

Even something as simple as learning how to ride a bike, ice-skate, or float requires us to let go and trust. The result is the acquisition of a new skill that previously seemed impossible. I should know since I did not learn to ride a bicycle or ice skate until I was in high school! I simply could not let go of my belief that we were meant to travel with our feet flat on the ground. It wasn't until a high school friend took me under his wing and forced me to grow up that I mastered these seemingly simple skills. It took a trusted friend to show me how to let go and believe that there were alternate ways of travelling through life. Both of those experiences provided me with a metaphor for life. Ever since, I have been challenged by the Lord to let go and to trust in matters bigger than bike riding and ice skating. Those times I held on refusing to let go simply prolonged my frustration and led to nowhere. Those times I successfully surrendered, I experienced conversion.

Learning to love our enemies, turn our cheeks, love others as ourselves, wash feet, and lay down our lives are all complex new skills that require us to let go of old ways of seeing and behaving. When we succeed at seeing things the way Jesus sees things, we experience the good news that frees us from ways that lead to death in favor of ways that lead to life! The good news is that *our* eyes can be opened to recognize the risen Christ, leading to a joy that makes our lives complete, restores hope, removes fear and anxiety, replaces anger with love, hatred with forgiveness, and emptiness with fullness of life. It is only when we let go of our hurts, angers, fears, doubts, and anxieties that our hands are free to embrace Jesus' cross that leads to new life.

The Anatomy of a Conversion

So, just how does a conversion happen? What does a conversion "look like?" Bernard Tyrell, author of *Christotherapy II*, explains that when we experience conversion, we, "like the disciples of Luke's Emmaus story, are gradually led by God to recognize and acknowledge a meaning in events and sufferings of the past which up to that point had seemed to be absurd and totally apart from any divine guidance. The facts of the past are not changed but they take on a new significance in the light of the resurrection-like experience of ongoing psychological conversion."[14]

The Bible is another good place to look for descriptions of conversion. Scripture is filled with stories of people who experienced conversion. In fact, the story of any significant biblical character is first and foremost a story of conversion. Abraham and Sarah overcame their conviction that they were too old. Moses overcame his belief that he was a "nobody" and a poor speaker. Jeremiah overcame his fear that he was too young. Jonah came to the conclusion that life onshore was better than in the belly of the whale. Mary overcame her doubts that new life within her was possible without an intimate relationship. Jesus overcame the temptation to be self-centered and self-serving. The list goes on.

Perhaps the most famous conversion story in scripture, however, is the story of Saul's conversion on the road to Damascus. Like the two disciples headed to Emmaus, Saul's conversion takes place on the road. (The biblical authors seem to recognize that as we journey along life's road, we are challenged to see in new and different ways.) At first glance, Saul's conversion seems immediate and sudden: he is knocked to the ground by a blinding light and gets up a changed man. He immediately lets go of his murderous thoughts and proceeds to preach the gospel.

A closer look at the story reveals a much more gradual process. Saul receives his mandate to persecute the Christians from the high priest and elders (Acts 22:5). Yet one of them, Gamaliel, at whose feet Saul had sat (Acts 22:3), had warned against the persecutions (Acts 5:34). The same Saul who was determined to carry out the persecutions against the Christians no doubt had moments of hesitation when, in his head, he heard the voice of his wise and respected teacher Gamaliel warning him *not* to proceed.

On the road to Damascus (Acts 9:1-19), Saul encountered a great light and was thrown to the ground. He heard a voice saying, "Saul, Saul, why are you persecuting me?" Upon asking who the voice was, Saul learned it was Jesus. As a result of this experience, Saul is blinded. He can no longer see as he once did. At the same time, he has no new vision—only darkness.

This experience continues for three days and three nights (a biblically symbolic period of time) until a disciple of Christ named Ananias comes to him with a vision. Laying hands upon Saul, he tells him, "Saul, my brother, the Lord has sent me, Jesus who appeared to you on the way by which you came, *that you may regain your sight* and be filled with the Holy Spirit" (Acts 9:17). Immediately, his eyes are opened and he is able to see, upon which he is baptized. The story tells us that he "stayed some days with the disciples in Damascus" (Acts 9:19) no doubt acquiring this new vision that eventually leads him to proclaim the good news to others. In all, this experience takes only a few paragraphs of scripture. In reality, the story indicates that the experience stretched out over some time.

For some of us conversion comes as a bolt of lightning, knocking us to the ground and lifting us up as a new person. For most, however, conversion is more gradual and subtle. Whatever the case, if we were to outline the anatomy of a conversion, the following ingredients would be present:

- *The experience of a "restlessness" or "inner ache."* Saul could not sit still, but needed to engage in some kind of action to bring meaning into his life. He chose to engage in active persecution of the Christians.
- *A period of time in which one investigates or explores as an attempt to fill the void.* Often these attempts are unhealthy and even lead to addictions. Saul certainly attempted to fill the void in his life by pursuing a path of violence.
- *A time of struggle.* Perhaps Saul was experiencing this within himself on the road to Damascus, struggling with the conflicting messages he had received from the elders and his teacher Gamaliel.
- *The "collapse" of one's world as one defines it.* For Saul, this was the experience of being knocked to the ground. In twelve-step programs, this is referred to as the experience of powerlessness or hitting rock bottom. This admission of powerlessness is the first step and a prerequisite to moving on in the twelve-step healing process. Later, Paul would boast of his powerless moments, saying that "when I am weak, then I am strong" (2 Cor 12:10). Paul refers to life before his conversion as "life in the flesh" and this new way of seeing as "life in the Spirit."
- *Surrender and the birth of a new vision.* Saul surrenders—he is literally taken by the hand and led to Damascus. He lets go of his old way of seeing and living but remains in the dark until Ananias, a disciple of Christ, helps him to see as Christ sees. Later, Paul would write of his experience and devote himself to sharing the Christian vision with others. Like the excited reader who sees the "magic eye" images pop out of the book for the first time, Paul cannot contain his euphoria over his new

vision but rushes out to invite others to see it as well. This is the essence of evangelization, a ministry which we are called to share.

When we journey to Emmaus, eventually we reach a fork in the road. One way leads us in circles where we repeatedly see and speak of the same things over and over. The other way leads us in a direction that will open our eyes to things we have never seen before. The moment at which we stand before that fork in the road is what we would call a moment of *crisis*. Hospitals refer to someone's condition as *critical* when there is an equal chance of survival or death. As we face the many crises of our ministry, we too have an equal chance of survival (new life) or death. The Lord tells us in Deuteronomy, "I have set before you life and death, the blessing and the curse. Choose life, then, that you and your descendants may live" (30:19). Living a life of fear, anxiety, doubt, anger, and hopelessness is truly a curse. I don't know about you, but I choose life!

Renewing Your Vision

Conversion is the process by which we renew our vision. At times, this process is painfully thrust upon us as a result of tragedy or misfortune. At other times, we can proactively conspire with the Lord to bring about our own conversion as we do each year during the season of Lent. While two different paths are taken, the end result is the same: transformation of one's life through acquisition of a new way of seeing.

By following the pattern set forth in the Emmaus story, we can discern some strategies for opening ourselves up to the possibility of conversion and the renewal of our vision for ministry and life. As you work the Emmaus story pattern, take these five strategies to heart:

1. Don't walk alone. Not only did the two disciples walk together, but they welcomed the stranger on the road to enter into their midst. In our own ministry, we all too often become "lone rangers." This is especially true when we become beleaguered. We tend to isolate ourselves out of fear of being hurt even more than we already have been. The disciples on the road could easily have given the Lord the brush off when he approached them and asked them what they were talking about. Instead, they opened themselves up to the possibility of a brand new relationship. More importantly, they opened themselves up to walk with, not just anyone, but Jesus.

To walk with the Lord is a prerequisite for renewing our vision, for in his book *Redemptive Intimacy*, Dick Westley questions, "But how can I tell if I am really 'walking with the Lord?"[15] Easily enough. To walk with the Lord is to have the very same effect on people that he did. After encountering us, do people feel freer, fear less, walk taller, think nobler, sing more joyfully, and feel more alive than ever before? Do we present an enhancing presence to our world?" If the answer is "Yes!" than we are on our way to renewing our vision!

2. Know when to "pull off the road." If you have ever driven a long distance by yourself, you know that you eventually reach a point where your eyes get so heavy or it's getting so dark that you need to pull off the road and take a rest. The disciples on the road saw that it was getting dark and knew a deserted road was no place to be in the dark. Darkness was considered the place where demons lurked.

In our own ministry, we need to recognize where the demons lurk and when it would be wise to "pull off the road." Then we need to do it! In the rock-opera *Jesus Christ Superstar*, the character of Jesus sings the lines, "And you think I could sleep well tonight? Let the world turn without me tonight?" to which the character of Mary Magdalene responds, "Close your eyes and relax, think of nothing tonight. Everything's alright, yes, everything's alright." One of the first steps in renewing our vision is to admit that it might be wise to pull off the road and let the world turn without us trying to push it every step of the way.

3. Invite the Lord in. Once again, the disciples on the road could have dismissed Jesus when he acted as though he meant to continue on. They made a very wise choice, however. They invited him in. Jesus always stands ready to assist us in renewing our vision. The problem is that sometimes we let him go on his way. We shut the door while we remain inside alone with our fears, hurts, and anxieties. It is precisely when we are mired in the loss of vision that we need to invite the Lord into our lives.

At times like these, our prayer may seem very strained. In fact, we may find that we are not praying at all. If this is the case, then our prayer should simply be a prayer of invitation to Jesus: "Please Lord, stay with me for it is growing dark." We need not have lengthy or profound words for our prayer. At times like this, we simply need to pray for the grace we need to see more clearly.

4. Show hospitality. The two disciples on the road showed generous hospitality to the stranger who was Jesus. Not only did they offer to protect him from the dangers of the darkened desert road, they also welcomed him to their table to share a meal. In this act of hospitality, their eyes are opened and they recognize the presence of the Lord. Robert Karris writes that, "Disciples who entertain the stranger will have their eyes opened. The lordship of Jesus is . . . attained through . . . an act of hospitality."[16] Each year during Lent, my family and I volunteer at a shelter for abused women where we serve the evening meal. At such a busy time of the year, when I tend to lose any ability to focus properly, this opportunity to provide some simple hospitality restores my sight and helps me to once again recognize where it is that I can find Jesus.

5. Allow Jesus to feed you. It is interesting to note that in the Emmaus story, the disciples invite Jesus to stay with them for dinner. Yet, *Jesus* is the one who takes the bread, pronounces the blessing, breaks it, and distributes it. The guest has become the host. It is this act that finally opens the eyes of the disciples: the recognition that it is the risen

Jesus who provides the nourishment needed for the journey.

Often, the only reason our vision is clouded or out of focus is because we have lost sight of who it is that feeds and sustains us. John Shea describes this phenomenon well in the beginning of a wonderful story of a brief exchange between Peter and Jesus:

> It is known by everyone who cares to know that the Lord Jesus and St. Peter used to repair to the local tavern after a hard day of ministry to break bread and drink wine together. On a certain rainy night, St. Peter turned to the Lord Jesus and grinned. "We're doing real good."
>
> "We?" said the Lord Jesus.
>
> Peter was silent. "All right, you're doing real good," he finally said.
>
> "Me?" said the Lord Jesus.
>
> Peter pondered a second time. "All right, God's doing real good," he finally admitted.
>
> But the Lord Jesus saw how reluctant St. Peter was to admit the source of all goodness.[17]

Ultimately, the key to renewing our vision for ministry is to recognize day in and day out that it is the Lord who gives us our daily bread. Perhaps the best therapy for renewing one's vision for ministry is simply to give praise to the Lord who is the source of all goodness. It is no coincidence the eucharistic prayer begins with the phrase, "Lord, *you* are holy indeed, the fountain of all holiness." These words remind us that the Lord is the host of the meal that restores sight.

In *The Resurrection According to Matthew, Mark and Luke*, Norman Perrin writes, "A last thing to be noted about the Emmaus road narrative is that there is a strong emphasis upon the Eucharist in it. Luke is telling his readers that the risen Lord can be known to them, as he became known to these two disciples, in the Eucharist."[18] Ultimately, the eucharist is our only salvation for renewing our vision for ministry, for it is in the eucharist that we give thanks and praise to the One who feeds us and restores our sight.

Where Did He Go . . . and Why?

Perhaps the most puzzling and troublesome line of the Emmaus story is the phrase that says, ". . . but he vanished from their sight." I always thought this part of the story was frustrating. We wait so long for these two lost souls to recognize that it is Jesus who is in their midst, and the very second that they do, he disappears! What is going on here? How are we to react?

First, I think it is important to take our cue from the two disciples themselves. When Jesus vanished from their sight, we might expect that the episode would come to a grinding halt and they would say something like, "Here we go again! Why does this always happen to us? Just our luck!" Instead, Luke tells us that they jump up from the table and hurry back to Jerusalem (more on that soon). The two disciples are telling us that this line is not to be taken as a disappointment, but somehow is integral to a renewed vision for ministry. This is crucial to all of us who read this story today and wonder where it is that we can find Jesus. The Emmaus story makes it clear: we do not need to have Jesus walking about in the flesh when he is present to us in the eucharist.

Which leads to a second point. What the two disciples realize is that just when they think they have Jesus in their grasp, he eludes them. In other words, we can never think that we've got Jesus figured out—he is greater than anything we can imagine! As soon as we think we've got our mind wrapped around the Lord, he transcends. This should not be a disappointment but rather a help for us to keep our vision for ministry clear. We proclaim a risen Jesus who is present and in our midst and yet, beyond our control. In the eucharist, we do not capture, control, or manipulate Jesus; we only get a glimpse or a taste of his awesome power that is present to us and yet somehow transcends us.

Merciful Father,

may these mysteries

give us new purpose

and bring us to

a new life in you.

—*The Sacramentary,* Prayer After Communion,
Wednesday of the Second Week of Easter

QUESTIONS FOR REFLECTION

- What is your favorite gospel passage of Jesus that deals with sight or blindness?
- What was an eye-opening (conversion) experience in your life? How did you come to see in a whole new way?
- In what way do you presently need the power of conversion? In what area of your life do you need to *repent*?
- What are you finding difficult to let go of at this time? What is something you have already let go of in your life?
- When did you experience a moment of crisis in your life? How did it transform you?
- What can you concretely do to renew your vision?
- What is an area of your life or ministry where you need to "pull off the road" for a while?
- Into what part of your life do you need to invite the Lord?
- How does Jesus feed you? What role does the eucharist play in your life and ministry?
- What does it mean to you that Jesus vanished in the Emmaus story?

INSIGHT

Salvation invisibly accompanies us along our way. God is always very near to a man through the various ages of life; but man's eyes are closed and he is not quite aware of it, he does not look closely enough, for he desires, he hankers and is so busy. Just as one can tell time by the shadow an object casts, so can one determine a person's maturity according to how close to him he thinks God is. Youth and adulthood run their course; it is not until evening comes and days decline that one understands that God is closer than all else, although one has not appreciated that fact.

—Soren Kierkegaard[19]

SCRIPTURE FOR PRAYER

> *Hear my voice, Lord, when I call;*
> *have mercy on me and answer me.*
> *"Come," says my heart, "seek God's face";*
> *your face, Lord, do I seek!*

—Psalm 27:7-8

7
Renewing Our Energy
"Were Not Our Hearts Burning?"

Then they said to each other, "Were not our hearts burning within us while he spoke to us on the way and opened the scriptures to us?"

—Luke 24:32

A Delayed Reaction

Does it ever take you a little while to figure out the punch line of a joke? Someone may have told the joke some time ago and then, in the middle of another conversation, you have a delayed reaction and blurt out, "Oh, *now* I get it!"

The two disciples on the road to Emmaus had such a delayed reaction to Jesus' earlier discussion of the scriptures while they walked the road. Recall that after the two had unloaded their heavy burdens on Jesus' bent ear, the Lord proceeded to interpret for them, beginning with Moses and all the prophets, everything that referred to him in all the scriptures. His words stirred something within them, but they couldn't put their finger on it. All they knew was that they were hungry and needed to stop for some food. It was only during the meal, when words were put aside and actions were allowed to speak, did the insight occur.

After participating in a meal that opened their eyes, the hearts and minds of the two disciples were now opened as well. Sign and symbol now brought meaning to the words. Suddenly, both the words Jesus spoke that afternoon and the world they were living in took on a whole new light. Their hearts and minds blurted out, "Oh, now I get it!" to that which their eyes had already recognized.

Two Kinds of Heartburn

When I was growing up, I had the privilege of working in my dad's pharmacy. To this day, in my basement, I keep momentos on display of our little corner drugstore once known as Paprocki Pharmacy. My collection includes a line of products that bear the Paprocki name: cough medicines, analgesic balms, and cold tablets. One of my favorites, however, is a bottle of white powder labeled *Paprocki's Antacid Powder*. The label proudly proclaims that this medicine is "for the relief of digestive distress due to gastric acidity and relieves heartburn, sour stomach, acid eructations, hyper-acidity, and belching." Customers coming into the store would describe all sorts of stomach ailments to my dad who would then confidently dispense a bottle of *Paprocki's Antacid Powder* to the soon-to-be-satisfied patron. No doubt, if my dad had heard the two disciples on the road to Emmaus exclaim, "were not our hearts burning within us?" he would have promptly dispensed some *Paprocki's Antacid Powder* to take care of their "heartburn."

All of this brings us to the conclusion that there are two types of heartburn—the bad kind and the good kind. The good kind of heartburn is that feeling we get when we hear, see, read, or experience something that inspires us. We may not know exactly what we intend to do with the newfound inspiration, but we simply feel charged up or on fire. While many of us take a variety of medications to get rid of the bad kind of heartburn, I'm sure we would give anything to find a way to bottle and keep the good kind.

The disciples experienced this good kind of heartburn when Jesus explained the scriptures to them on the road to Emmaus. No one had ever interpreted scripture for them like this before. Jesus was able to open their eyes to a whole new way of seeing salvation. His "liturgy of the word" on the road set the table for the "liturgy of the eucharist" that would follow that very evening. Word and Sacrament combined to open up the eyes, minds, and hearts of the disciples. The fire that they began to feel in their hearts as Jesus interpreted scripture for them now burst forth into a raging inferno while at table. Their hearts were burning with the good kind of heartburn for which no remedy is sought—only the opportunity to spread their condition to others!

Passion for Ministry

This "fire" that the disciples felt burning within their hearts is an indication of the presence of the Holy Spirit. To the old saying, "where there's smoke, there's fire," can be added: "where there's fire, there's the Holy Spirit!" In fact, to be a disciple of Christ means to be "on fire" with the power of the risen Christ. It is no coincidence that on the night we celebrate the baptisms of new Christians at the Easter Vigil, we begin with the lighting of FIRE! The blessing of the Paschal candle includes the words, "Make this new fire holy and *inflame us* with new hope."

At various times in our lives, we have been "on fire" for Christ. For some of us, it was long ago. For others, the fire is still burning. Whatever the case, that fire can best be described as a *passion* for our ministry. At various times we approach our ministry with this passion or zeal that fuels our every move and spurs us on to work long hours with great enthusiasm and creativity. Our "fire" grows in intensity. For some, listening to an outstanding preacher may fuel it. For others, it may be a result of sharing in a spiritual companioning relationship or from reading scripture. The fire may come from meditation or listening to sacred music or from a very prayerful celebration of the eucharist. Or, it may come from participating in an excellent catechetical seminar, class, or workshop. The fire may come about as the result of a profound life experience or as subtly as in a whisper. However it happens, the presence of God touches us and sets our hearts on fire, creating within us a passion for spreading the good news!

The Passionate Paul

Where can we find an example of this passion for spreading the gospel? Again St. Paul is the model. The former Saul of Tarsus was so passionate for the good news that he was willing to suffer pain and imprisonment for its sake. Paul's passion stemmed from a profound awareness that the risen Christ was in his midst and had touched his life in a transforming way. This passion is expressed in his letters as he attempts to spread his zeal for the gospel to others. St. Paul's passion is perhaps best summed up in his second letter to the Corinthians:

Therefore, since we have this ministry through the mercy shown us, we are not discouraged. We are afflicted in every way, but not constrained; perplexed but not driven to despair; persecuted but not abandoned; struck down but not destroyed (4:1, 8-9).

Paul's passion for the gospel of Jesus allows him to rise above any and all hardships. This same tireless passion was also expressed in his letter to the Philippians; he writes,

Just one thing: forgetting what lies behind but straining forward to what lies ahead, I continue my pursuit toward the goal, the prize of God's upward calling in Christ Jesus (3:13-14).

Talk about passion!

Rea McDonnell addressed the passion of St. Paul, writing that "his passion burned among his contemporaries in the early church, and continues to energize teachers, preachers and missionaries, the apostles and evangelists of today. Paul's passion means not only his life-long suffering on behalf of Christ and Christ's churches, but also his deep and long-lasting emotion and his focused desire that Christ be preached to the nations."[20] It is this same fire that must burn within us if we are to properly serve as ministers of the gospel.

As disciples of Christ, we are called to be passionate! At times, however, the flame within us flickers and goes weak. When this happens, passion gives way to apathy. It is no coincidence that we refer to this experience as *burnout*. When the fire within us burns out, we are in danger of becoming the very antithesis of what it means to be a disciple of Christ. Without passion, we simply cannot effectively proclaim the passion, death and resurrection of Jesus. We need to confront the apathy or lack of passion in our life and in our ministry if we are to carry the good news to all nations.

Confronting Apathy

In *Ministry Burnout*, author John Sanford describes burnout in the following ways:

- We must imagine a man or woman who has been devoured from within by fiery energy until, like a gutted house, nothing is left.
- Or we may imagine a person who once carried a current of psychic energy but now, like a burned out electrical conductor, cannot supply power anymore.
- Or an individual who, like a burned out forest, feels that her power to renew herself has been destroyed.[21]

The result of this burned out feeling is *apathy*. The word apathy comes from the Greek *a-pathea* meaning "without feeling." Stoic philosophy believed that to be without feeling or emotion was one of the highest achievable attributes. This was one of the challenges that the passionate Paul faced in his ministry, since stoicism was prevalent in many of the Greek-speaking audiences he preached to. When we experience burnout, we become stoic or without feeling. We need to re-ignite the fire within.

Some years ago, after a backyard barbecue, I let the charcoal burn out—or so I thought. I waited a few hours, packed up the charcoal in aluminum foil, and tossed it into the garbage can. A few hours later, I smelled something burning. I looked out the window and saw my garbage can in flames. It seems those charcoals still had some life in them! The same is true of us when we experience burnout. It may seem as though we have nothing left to give. Yet, the fire of the Holy Spirit never completely goes out. With some embers still glowing, the fire can be rekindled.

In Nathaniel Branden's article "Passion and Soulfulness," he writes that two things are needed to keep the inner fire alive: "an ability to appreciate the positives in our life and a commitment to action." Both of these are gifts of the Holy Spirit. The gift of wonder and awe leads us to appreciate the positive power of God in our lives. The gift of fortitude leads us to make commitments to action despite obstacles. Branden adds, "I believe that the worst of all spiritual defeats is to lose enthusiasm for life's possibilities. Even when our life is most difficult, it is important to remember that something within us is keeping us alive—the life force—that lifts us, energizes us, pulls us back sometimes from the abyss of despair. True spirituality does not exist without love of life."[22]

Through the power of the Holy Spirit, the fire within us can become rekindled. If you are feeling apathetic in your ministry or are experiencing burnout, don't give up! The spark within you can and will be ignited once again by the Holy Spirit. In the words of Dante, "A mighty flame followeth a tiny spark." Our prayer must remain the prayer of the words sung in the *Exsultet* at the Easter Vigil: "May the Morning Star which never sets find this flame still burning!"

Leave Your Apathy at the Door

Scripture tells us that there is no place for apathy in our spiritual lives. As the book of Proverbs puts quite bluntly: "As vinegar to the teeth, and smoke to the eyes, is the *sluggard* to those who use him as a messenger" (10:26). The dictionary defines sluggard as one "who is habitually lazy or idle; sluggish." We may not be lazy but at times, we do become sluggish and apathetic in our ministry. We need to remember that *we* are God's messengers. The message we are delivering is one of great power and joy. What aftertaste do we leave? Hopefully, not one of "vinegar to the teeth!"

In another astonishingly blunt passage, God speaks to those who are mired in apathy with the following warning: "I know your works; I know that you are neither cold nor hot. I wish you were either cold or hot. So because you are *lukewarm*, neither hot nor cold, I will spit you out of my mouth" (Rev 3:15-16). Jesus himself is quite clear on this matter when he says, "I have come to set the earth on fire and how I wish it were already blazing!" (Lk 12:49). The message for us is loud and clear: if we are experiencing apathy or burnout in our ministry, we need to do something about it. We cannot continue in a malaise. The Word of God deserves nothing but our best. At times like this, we need to do all that we can to surrender to the power of the Holy Spirit and allow the fire to consume us once again and set us on fire. To paraphrase a famous song by *The Doors* from the 1960s, we need to sing out, "Come on, *Spirit*, light my fire!"

The feast of Pentecost is a feast of fire. The story of the descent of the Holy Spirit tells us that the disciples were consumed with the Holy Spirit and that "tongues as of fire . . . parted and came to rest on each of them" (Acts 2:3). Each of us desires and needs an experience of Pentecost in our own lives. We need not wait until the liturgical feast of Pentecost, however, for this to happen. The fire of the Holy Spirit cannot be programmed according to a calendar. As in the words of the great hymn, we must pray: "Come Holy Ghost, creator blest, and in our hearts take up thy rest!"

Re-Charging Your Batteries

Think of the many appliances you have in your house that need to have batteries either replaced or recharged:

- smoke detector
- cell phone
- video camera
- garden shears
- flashlights
- laptop computer
- portable vacuum
- alarm clocks

We recognize that, from time to time, we need to change the batteries or plug the device into an electrical outlet to get it recharged. Why not apply the same wisdom to our own lives? For some reason, we think that we can go on and on without taking a break to recharge our own "batteries." In *The Seven Habits of Highly Effective People*, Steven Covey uses the famous children's fable of the goose that laid the golden egg to illustrate this important point. In that story, the farmer who discovers that his goose lays golden eggs becomes greedy and kills the goose in order to get all of the eggs at once. Of course, when he cuts the goose open, it is empty. The farmer loses not only his gold, but also the goose that produced it. Covey says that "most people see effectiveness from the golden egg paradigm: the more you produce, the more you do, the more effective you are. But as this story shows, true effectiveness is a function of two things: what is produced (golden eggs) and the producing asset or capacity to produce (the goose)."[23] Needless to say, we need to be sure we don't "kill" our own goose. Several suggestions follow:

Read the Bible. Often our apathy and burnout stems from the feeling that we are alone and isolated. When we read scripture, we find not only that God is with us, but that we are part of a greater story that provides a context for our own personal experience. Reading scripture helps us to see our experience in a whole new way—and it gives the good kind of heartburn.

Listen to an audio presentation of a good speaker. One of the best ways to get fired up is to listen to a fiery speaker or preacher. Go to the religious goods store or sift through a catalogue to find inspirational or motivational tapes or CDs from speakers you really enjoy. Listen to them in your car when you drive and allow their fire to ignite you.

Take a few hours off and get out into nature. Our energy can be renewed without the use of caffeine or nicotine! Nature provides us with an energizing force that cannot be equaled. Too often, we are trapped in our concrete jungles where fresh air and sunlight are limited. Get out to an area where you can allow nature to refresh you. Scripture tells us that Jesus often went off by himself to an out of the way place to renew himself. As his disciples, we do him no honor by thinking we never need to take a break.

Attend a good workshop, seminar, or course. Many of us are required to complete ongoing formation. Don't think of this as a hoop to jump through or more time that you are giving up to someone else. Instead, think of it as a chance to massage your spirit. Treat yourself to a good experience that will enhance your life and ministry, renew your vision, and rekindle your passion for ministry.

Be proactive in planning your vacation and days off. I have a friend who did not take a vacation for several years because "there was just too much going on at the parish."

Nonsense! Sit down with your calendar now and block out the times during the year when you will disappear for a day off or a longer vacation. This includes planning an occasional afternoon off. Write those days into your calendar. When someone asks if you are available, you can say, "No, I will be busy that day." Only *you* will know that you will be busy "doing nothing."

Attend a purely social event. Not every event we attend needs to be connected with religion or church. Take some time out to attend something that is purely social (e.g., a concert, a cookout, etc.) where the talk will not be connected with your work. This gives you a chance to take off all of the various hats you wear in your ministry and just be yourself.

Take thirty minutes for a walk or some stretching. Many of us use the breaks provided to us in our daily schedule to grab a cup of coffee and a donut. Instead of loading up on calories, sugar, and caffeine, take a brisk walk to break up your day or find a place to do some simple stretching exercises. Stretching gets the blood flowing and renews your energy.

Do some service. Service is especially effective if your work tends to be administrative or clerical. When planning and implementing programs, we often do not get a sense of accomplishment. Doing some type of direct service (e.g., volunteering at a soup kitchen, etc.) provides us with an opportunity to directly touch others' lives and allow the Spirit within those we serve to rekindle the Spirit within us.

Light a candle in your workspace and play reflective music. I'm not going to get "new age" on you here, but it can be energizing to turn off the bright fluorescent lights and do your work in a more reflective setting. Rekindling the flame does not have to involve anything loud or noisy. Quiet may be just what you need to recharge your batteries. (P.S. Check your local fire regulations!)

Turn off the TV. Watching television is a passive activity that reinforces the feeling of boredom and apathy. Yet, studies show that Americans are watching five to six hours of television per day on average. One way to recharge your batteries is to turn off the TV, put on some music, and read a good book. Or, go out to sit on the back porch and watch the birds of the air (see page 62)!

Break up routine and monotony. Doing the same thing in the same way, day in and day out, often exacerbates apathy. One way to energize yourself is to break up your daily routine: take a new route to work, alter your schedule, go out to lunch if you usually eat in, eat in if you always go out.

Sleep. Simply put, without enough sleep, we have no hope of recharging our batteries. A solid eight hours of sleep provides us with enough time to renew our energy for a new day. If your work simply does not allow you to get enough sleep, you need to take a serious look at your job description and decide what needs to go. If something doesn't, you will!

Compete. Getting involved in some sort of competition (athletic or hobby) provides a forum for engaging our energy, which may be lying fallow within us. Getting fired up about life will help us get fired up about our ministry.

Keep holy the Sabbath. The third commandment is there for a reason. God knows that one of the best ways to be renewed is to stop doing and just *be!* If God could take a day off after completing all of creation, it is blasphemy for us to think we can do better by working non-stop.

Eucharist. The eucharist is intended to set your lives on fire. To spice up your liturgical life, try occasionally visiting another parish for Mass. While my own parish has a wonderful liturgy program, my family and I will occasionally attend Mass at an African-American parish not far from our home where the spirit of praise and thanksgiving is always evident. African-American spirituality leaves no room for apathy and expresses the energy and enthusiasm we all need to be disciples in Christ.

These are only a few suggestions for renewing our energy for the journey. The important thing to remember is that while *we* often become apathetic and lose our energy, God never grows weary. For those of us who are weary, Jesus extends the following invitation: "Come to me, all you who labor and are burdened, and I will give you rest" (Mt 11:28). Sounds like a nice invitation. We need to respond. In fact, resisting the invitation only prolongs the frustration. The prophet Jeremiah, who grew weary of suffering and rejection, tried to hang up his prophetic jersey: "I say to myself, I will not mention him, I will speak in his name no more. But then it becomes like fire burning in my heart, imprisoned in my bones; I grow weary holding it in, I cannot endure it" (Jer 20:9). Like Paul, once consumed by the Holy Spirit, we become "prisoners of Christ!"

A Face Like Moses

The book of Exodus tells us that when Moses came down from the mountaintop, his face was radiant from his encounter with the Lord (34:29). Louis Savary tells us that "when Moses realized that he was alive with God's life, it burst forth for all to see. He had beheld the glory of the Lord and it was reflected in his face."[24] When we are filled with the Spirit, like Moses, the glory of the Lord will be reflected in our faces. We must never forget to ask the Lord to fill us with the Holy Spirit who will blow on the embers within our hearts and re-ignite the fires of passion for proclaiming the good news!

May that fire which hovered over the disciples
as tongues of flame
burn all evil from your hearts
and make them glow with pure light.

—*The Sacramentary*,
Solemn Blessing, Holy Spirit

QUESTIONS FOR REFLECTION

- Describe a time when were you "on fire" for the gospel.
- What gives you the "good kind" of heartburn? What "sets you on fire?"
- What are you most passionate about in your life? In your ministry? What are you experiencing apathy over?
- How is St. Paul a model of passion for ministry?
- What role does the Holy Spirit play in your life and ministry? What role can the Holy Spirit play?
- How do you "recharge your batteries?" What do you do to renew your energy?
- Who is "Moses" in your life (e.g., someone whose face "bursts forth" with the radiance of God's life)? How can your face reflect God's glory?

INSIGHT

This purgative and loving knowledge or divine light we are speaking of, has the same effect on the soul that fire has on a log of wood. The soul is purged and prepared for union with the divine light just as the wood is prepared for transformation into the fire. Fire, when applied to wood, first dehumidifies it, dispelling all moisture and making it give off any water it contains. Then it gradually turns the wood black, makes it dark and ugly, and even causes it to emit a bad odor. By drying out the wood, the fire brings to light and expels all those ugly and dark accidents which are contrary to fire. Finally, by heating and enkindling it from without, the fire transforms the wood into itself and makes it as beautiful as it is itself.

—St. John of the Cross[25]

SCRIPTURE FOR PRAYER

Do you not know
or have you not heard?
The Lord is the eternal God,
creator of the end of the earth.
He does not faint nor grow weary,
and his knowledge is beyond scrutiny.
He gives strength to the fainting;
for the weak he makes vigor abound.
They that hope in the Lord will renew
their strength;
they will soar as with eagles' wings;
They will run and not grow weary,
walk and not grow faint.

—Isaiah 40:28-29, 31

8

Renewing Our Commitment
"They Set Out at Once and Returned to Jerusalem"

So they set out at once and returned to Jerusalem
where they found gathered together the eleven and
those with them. . . .

—Luke 24:33

About-Face, Forward, March!

Funny how Emmaus didn't seem so important anymore. Just hours before, these two disciples were fleeing Jerusalem with the intention of never going back again. After their encounter with the risen Lord, however, they did an about-face, a complete 180 degree reversal. Without hesitation, they began marching, armed with new life, to the very place where they had previously encountered death and defeat. Their sense of fear was gone at the same time their sense of purpose and direction was restored. They had no idea what was waiting for them there or what might happen to them when they arrived. They simply knew that their hearts were on fire and that they had some amazingly good news to proclaim. The road from Emmaus *to* Jerusalem was somehow much shorter and less confusing than the road from Jerusalem to Emmaus. They were returning to the same place from whence they came, but they were not the same persons they once were. More importantly, they knew now that they were not alone and had never been alone.

What Are We Waiting For?

One of the symptoms of ministerial burnout is passivity. The idea of taking the initiative on anything is just completely overwhelming. Retreating to Emmaus is less of a plan than it is an escape. In order to renew our ministry, we need to embrace the concept of *proactivity*. The disciples on the road wasted no time in returning to Jerusalem after their encounter with the risen Lord. They were overcome with a sense of urgency and could not wait to bring their good news to the ends of the earth. In our own ministry, we, too, need to have this sense of urgency. When we are consumed with passion for our Lord Jesus Christ, there is not a moment to lose nor is there a reason to hesitate. The world around us is crying out for deliverance and now is the acceptable time.

Did the two disciples on the road have an idea of what they were going to do in Jerusalem? Did they sit down and work out a strategic plan? Did they form a committee to study the possible options? No! They proactively set out at once—prompted by the Holy Spirit—and formulated any necessary plans along the way.

At the same time, being proactive should not be confused with recklessness. In *A Passion For Excellence* Tom Peters and Nancy Austin differentiate being proactive from hurried sloppiness. They explain that "you must experiment and learn your way toward perfection/completion. 'Winners' are, above all, pragmatic non-blue-sky dreamers who live by one dictum: *try it now*." Their philosophy is that "setbacks—not sloppy foul-ups, but thoughtful missteps along the way—are considered to be normal. The winners are seen as people who persist."[26] This advice can be applied to our ministry as well. To quote the fiery World War II hero General George Patton: "A good plan . . . executed right now is far better than a perfect plan executed next week." To be proactive in our ministry is to move forward with a sense of urgency, honing our vision as we make progress.

Stephen Covey includes being proactive as one of his "seven habits of highly effective people" and explains that "it means that as human beings, we are responsible for our own lives. We have the responsibility and the initiative to make things happen." He also writes that proactive people "do not blame circumstances, conditions, or conditioning for their behavior," but instead choose responsibility or "response-ability."[27]

A close look at the two disciples on the road reveals that they underwent this type of transformation. Like them, we often become paralyzed by fear, anxiety, negativity, cynicism, and even exhaustion. Being proactive in ministry means moving ahead with renewed energy, taking the small steps, accepting but not dwelling upon our failures, and creating new opportunities, new hope, and new life.

Go Forth!

Every Sunday at Mass, when we recite our profession of faith, we utter the words, "we believe in *one holy catholic* and *apostolic* Church." These four words capture the essence and characteristics of our faith community. For our purposes here, I would like to focus on the word *apostolic*.

More often than not, we define apostolic as being able to trace our roots back to the twelve apostles. This is indeed an essential part of our faith. However, the word apostolic also carries another meaning. To be *apostolic* means to be "one who is sent" (from the Greek *apostellein*, meaning, "to send"). St. Paul considered himself an *apostle* of Jesus because he encountered the Lord on the road to Damascus and came away with a mandate to proclaim the gospel to the ends of the earth. Paul believed without a shadow of a doubt that he was commissioned by Christ himself in the same way that he had previously been commissioned by the Jewish elders to purify Judaism of the Christians. To be an apostolic church means to be a community of people who have encountered the Lord and have been commissioned through baptism to go forth and proclaim the good news!

The disciples on the road, after encountering the risen Lord, got up at once to go forth and tell their stories. Apostles of Jesus do not sit around and wait for something to happen—they go forth! It is no coincidence that the word we use to describe our eucharistic celebrations, namely the *Mass*, actually comes from the Latin word *missa*, that means, "sent." The last words proclaimed to us at Mass by the priest or deacon are, "Go forth, to love and serve the Lord." This is a mandate, not an invitation; a responsibility, not an option. Our response of "Thanks be to God" shows that we are thankful, not only for the blessings God has given us, but also for the opportunity to be sent forth to share the good news with others.

If we are stuck on the road to Emmaus, traveling in circles and getting nowhere, we are not truly acting as apostles of Jesus. We need to get up, go, and bring the Word of God to those places where it is most needed. We need to get beyond "maintenance" ministry and into "mission" ministry. Too often, we are in a passive mode, waiting for people to come to us. We keep waiting for the doorbells of our parish ministry centers to ring. Instead, we as a church need to get out and ring the doorbells of those who have yet to encounter the risen Lord and invite them into a whole new way of seeing and living.

A Mission Statement for Evangelization

When we minister as those who are sent, we are participating in the ministry known as *evangelization*. How appropriate that the pope who is credited with setting forth a vision for evangelization was named Paul! In 1975 Pope Paul VI published what many consider to be the magna carta of evangelization: *Evangelii Nuntiandi* ("On Evangelization in the Modern World"). This document serves as a mission statement for all of us who minister in the name of Jesus and are sent forth to proclaim his good news. The following quotation from *Evangelii Nuntiandi* serves as a rallying cry for apostles of Jesus everywhere to set out at once and preach the gospel:

Let us therefore preserve our fervor of spirit. Let us preserve the delightful and comforting joy of evangelizing, even when it is in tears that we must sow. May it mean for us—as it did for John the Baptist, for Peter and Paul, for the other Apostles and for a multitude of splendid evangelizers all through the Church's history—an interior enthusiasm that nobody and nothing can quench. And may the world of our time, which is searching, sometimes with anguish, sometimes with hope, be enabled to receive the good news not from evangelizers who are dejected, discouraged, impatient or anxious, but from ministers of the gospel whose lives glow with fervor, who have first received the joy of Christ, and who are willing to risk their lives so that the Kingdom may be proclaimed and the church established in the midst of the world.[28]

I recommend that anyone who is experiencing a malaise in his or her ministry, pick up this document and read it. You'll quickly come to realize that there is no such thing as a sitting-still apostle.

Personal Mission Statement

Evangelii Nuntiandi was promulgated on the tenth anniversary of the closing of the Second Vatican Council, a council that was a time of renewal for the church; an experience of conversion. The church embarked on a journey toward a renewed vision of herself and the world. This is what we need to do for ourselves. We need to have our own personal "Vatican II." A time set apart to take a close look at ourselves, open the windows, and let in some fresh air! A time to re-define who we are in relation to ourselves, others, and God.

The good news is that we don't have to wait for conversion to happen to us. With the help of the Holy Spirit, we can experience conversion at any time. Scripture tells us that the Holy Spirit led Jesus into the desert where he was tempted. Jesus didn't wait to be knocked to the ground; he chose to grapple with his conversion head on before forging ahead in his ministry with renewed commitment. We, too, can grapple with our own conversion and renew our commitment to ministry by taking a good hard look at who we are and who we hope to be. One suggestion for doing this is to sit down and compose a personal mission statement.

Stephen Covey encourages readers of *The Seven Habits of Highly Effective People* to compose their own mission statements in the same way that many corporations do. Covey says that a personal mission statement "focuses on what you want to be (character) and to do (contributions and achievements) and on the values or principles upon which being and doing are based."[29] Just as the Second Vatican Council inspired a new vision for evangelization, we too can compose a "document" that serves to renew our vision and act as the foundation and center of our lives. I wrote my own personal mission statement some years ago and share it here as an example.

My mission is to . . .
- recognize and appreciate my life as a gift from God.
- use my gifts wisely, unselfishly, and with integrity to love and serve others without seeking reward but to do so for the greater glory of God.
- embrace the present moment of life as the only reality.

To fulfill this mission, I must . . .
- regularly recognize and acknowledge my giftedness through reflection.
- make space to listen to God's will so as to avoid serving myself.
- care for my gifts through rest and exercise.
- use my gifts in service to others seeking no reward.
- seek reward only from the knowledge that I have been consistent with my principles.
- stretch beyond my comfort zones to participate in life.
- acknowledge that Jesus is Lord and make efforts to build my relationship with him.
- keep perspective focused on the greater good instead of on individual battles.
- exercise courage to struggle in individual battles when they serve the greater good.

These roles take priority in achieving my mission . . .
SELF—I can honor God best by becoming the person God intends me to be.

MATE—I choose to share my personal journey with my Jo who is my friend, lover, wife, and mother to my children. I commit myself to sharing the experience of life with her.

FATHER—I commit myself to Mike and Amy and offer my guidance, love, patience, discipline, friendship, and compassion. I recognize and respect their uniqueness and offer guidance with open hands. I assume responsibility for difficult times and embrace the good times.

FRIEND—I recognize my need to share in relationships with others and commit myself to move beyond the boundaries of my own life and allow others in.

SON/FAMILY—I recognize and appreciate all my parents and family have done to shape my life and commit to nourish and sustain those relationships.

MINISTER—I have been gifted by God with the ability to serve others in their spiritual formation through my role as a Catechetical Consultant, Pastoral Associate/DRE, author, and speaker. I commit myself to serving others in my ministry and offer my gifts to the people of God with humility for the sole purpose of building the body of Christ and bringing glory to God!

The experience of writing this personal mission statement (which I keep with my daily calendar) was a time of renewal for me. Each time I go back to look at it and update or revise it, I feel a sense not only of focus and clarity, but also renewed enthusiasm and zeal. Like the disciples on the road, when our vision is restored, we are compelled to set out at once and return to the "Jerusalems" of our ministry and renew our proclamation of the good news!

Returning After Exile

Was it wise for the disciples to return to Jerusalem? An old saying tells us that "you can never go home again." On the one hand, there is some wisdom in this. We can never return to the days of our youth or try to relive an experience exactly the way it once was. As Dick Westley writes, "We have all gone to class reunions, returned to the old neighborhood, gathered with friends from the past, and though there may be rare exceptions, most often we are painfully reminded of the fact that time does not stand still, that people and attitudes do change, and that nostalgia is one of the most unrealistic of human passions. We must either learn to live with our present sense of loss, or we must attempt to articulate and practice a spirituality that answers our needs in the present and yet is recognizable as an authentic way of walking with the Lord in faith."[30]

At the same time, like the disciples on the road, we *can* return to places where we previously experienced both great joy and great pain. Just as the disciples returned to Jerusalem, we too can return to our ministerial setting after a brief jaunt on the road to Emmaus. We must know, however, that we are returning with a new and renewed vision. We are not returning because we are gluttons for punishment, looking forward to hitting our heads against the wall again and again.

A contemporary definition of insanity is doing the same thing over and over again but expecting different results. We would truly be insane to return to a place where we experienced death unless we were bringing with us a vision for new life. When we encounter the risen Lord, we are capable of doing the impossible because we are no longer the same person, but, as St. Paul says, we are a "new creation" (2 Cor 5:17).

This return would not be unlike the return of the Israelites after their exile experience in Babylon. It *is* possible to "go home again" but it requires a re-interpretation of our previous experience. The people of Israel who once held the belief that they could have no existence without the Temple and the Holy City of Jerusalem needed to re-interpret this belief after they survived generations in exile and returned to a desolated city and destroyed Temple. They returned with great joy, but also with revised expectations and some hard-earned wisdom.

When *we* return to our ministry after a walk to Emmaus, we return older and wiser, and with a different set of expectations—not cynical and pessimistic, but hopeful and optimistic. In the language of spirituality, this is referred to as the "second naiveté" in which we regain a vision that sees the world with the hope and optimism of our youth and more wisdom than ever. Benedict Groeschel describes it in this way: "The faith of adolescence is based on clear ideas tentatively held until better explanations are found. Mature faith, according to St. John of the Cross, is the opposite. Instead of being tentative it is certain because the author of this faith is God."[31] We return to Jerusalem with a more mature faith that has been tested in fire, purged of impurities, and both strengthened and polished.

The Ability to Adjust

Some people never recover from painful experiences. Many of us know of people who died within a few short months of their spouse's death. The trauma of the event led them to lose their own desire to live. Others, however, follow up their grieving and mourning with healing and re-birth. It would seem that the secret for these people lies in their abilities to make adjustments.

The ability to adjust is what a Chicago Cubs broadcaster Steve Stone identified as the key to separating a good athlete from a superstar athlete. Stone insists that raw talent will only get you so far in any sport and that it is the ability to adjust that separates superstars from the ordinary, everyday players. Stone explains that once the pitchers in the league detect the strengths of a particular hitter, they no longer pitch to that strength. Thus, a hitter who likes to hit fastballs will soon see a steady diet of curveballs. What separates a great player from an ordinary player is the ability to adjust. A good fastball hitter must also learn to hit curveballs.

This ability to adjust was also one of the favorite themes of Michael Jordan's illustrious career with the Chicago Bulls. Quite often, the Bulls of the 1990s would look shaky in the first half of a game only to come out in the second half and blow the team away. Time and again, Jordan explained in post-game interviews that during halftime, the team reviewed what the opposing team was doing to them, and then simply made adjustments. The Bulls did not excel against just one type of team but were able to make adjustments to play against a variety of teams. The result was six championships in eight years—more than the Cubs have achieved in over 100 years!

In our ministry, the key to our success lies in our ability to adjust to situations. If we try to play the ministerial "game" without making adjustments to changing times and situations, we will lose our edge. Like the church of Vatican II, we need to read the signs of the times, make some adjustments, and get to work.

Renewing Your Commitment

The time has come for you to re-commit yourself to your ministry. As baptized Christians, we do this when we renew our baptismal vows, both at the Easter Vigil, and throughout the Easter season. After engaging in our lenten disciplines intended to regain our focus as apostles of Jesus, we emerge at Easter with a vision of new life, ready to be sent forth. Use these baptismal promises as a way to re-commit yourselves to your faith and your ministry. Make sure to answer "I do!"

Do you reject sin, so as to live in the freedom of God's children?

Do you reject the glamour of evil, and refuse to be mastered by sin?

Do you reject Satan, father of sin and prince of darkness?

Do you believe in God, the Father almighty, Creator of heaven and earth?

Do you believe in Jesus Christ, his only Son, our Lord, who was born of the Virgin Mary, was crucified, died, and was buried, rose from the dead, and is now seated at the right hand of the Father?

Do you believe in the Holy Spirit, the holy catholic church, the communion of saints, the forgiveness of sins, the resurrection of the body, and life everlasting?

God, the all powerful Father of our Lord Jesus Christ, has given us a new birth by water and the holy spirit, and forgiven all our sins.

May he also keep us faithful to our Lord Jesus Christ for ever and ever.

Amen.

With that in mind, go forth to love and serve the Lord!

Father,

you will your Church to be the sacrament of salvation
for all peoples.

Make us feel more urgently

the call to work for the salvation of all men,

until you have made us all one people.

Inspire the hearts of all your people

to continue the saving work of Christ everywhere

until the end of the world.

—*The Sacramentary*, Opening Prayer,
For the Spread of the Gospel

QUESTIONS FOR REFLECTION

- In what area of your ministry are you being too passive?
- When was a time when you were successfully proactive? What is an area of your ministry where you need to be more proactive?
- To be "apostolic" means to be sent. Where is the Lord sending you?
- What are three elements that would definitely be part of your mission statement?
- What "places" have you returned to in your ministry with a little more wisdom than you once had?
- When was a time you successfully made a major adjustment in your ministry?

INSIGHT

If the Bible is anything, it's the word of God's involvement in the action *of history. A great image of this is Mary's Visitation, as recorded in the first chapter of Luke. As I read this story, I was struck by how different her response was to what my response probably would have been. If I found out I was to be the mother of God, the first thing I would plan would be a thirty-day retreat or something. I'd say to myself, 'I gotta go into solitude and get it together and purify my motives and work this out theologically.'*

I would go inside my head. Yet read the passage. She is out of herself; she is free of her need to get it together. Immediately she set out for the hill country of Judea to help her cousin, whom she heard was pregnant, too. Here it is, the primacy of action. If your life is not moving toward practical action in this real, living world, with other people, with the not-me, don't trust your spirituality. But your engagement must happen in tandem with contemplation, the inner disengagement with ego and openness to God. Action and contemplation are the two polarities that regulate and balance the faith-filled life.

—Richard Rohr[32]

SCRIPTURE FOR PRAYER

*The desert and the parched land will exult;
    the steppe will rejoice and bloom.
They will bloom with abundant flowers,
    and rejoice with joyful song.
Strengthen the hands that are feeble,
    make firm the knees that are weak.
Say to those whose hearts are frightened:
    Be strong, fear not!
Here is your God,
    he comes with vindication;
With divine recompense
    he comes to save you.
Those whom the Lord has ransomed will return
And enter Zion singing,
Crowned with everlasting joy.*

—Isaiah 35:1-2a, 3-4, 10

9
Renewing Our Ministry
"The Lord Has Truly Been Raised!"

. . . they found gathered together the eleven and those with them who were saying, "The Lord has truly been raised and has appeared to Simon!" Then the two recounted what had taken place on the way and how he was made known to them in the breaking of the bread.

—Luke 24:33-35

Home Again

It had been a long journey for the two disciples. They had set out with a destination leading to nowhere. They had traveled in circles, covering the same painful terrain over and over again. They had encountered a stranger who took the time to listen to their pain and despair and then offered them a totally different perspective on their experience. As they listened to him explain the scriptures, they developed a mysteriously good kind of heartburn.

Fearful of being alone in the dark, they had persuaded the stranger to stay with them and eat. They shared a familiar meal, and when the bread was broken, their eyes were miraculously opened with a vision of new life. Suddenly they were no longer lost, no longer afraid, no longer in despair, no longer hungry, no longer tired, and no longer alone. In their haste to return to Jerusalem, they no doubt left their luggage at the Emmaus inn where they were also leaving behind some painful emotional baggage. When they got back to Jerusalem, they discovered that the Lord had been busy opening the eyeballs of others that had also previously fled in their haste to forget Jerusalem for various destinations as un-exotic as Emmaus. Now that they were "back," there was only one thing left to do: *tell the story to others.*

The Lord Has Truly Been Raised

There is only one thing to do when we encounter the risen Lord: SHOUT ABOUT IT! In our ministry, we are sent forth to proclaim the good news that Jesus has conquered all things that lead to death, and that he lives and reigns forever. Each of us has our own style for doing this. To proclaim that "Jesus is Lord" does not require that we suddenly change our persona and go about shouting at the top of our lungs like a TV evangelist.

Several years ago, the Office for Catechesis of the Archdiocese of Chicago sponsored a two-day catechetical conference attended by several thousand people. The conference featured two keynote speakers whose delivery styles were as different as night and day. On the first day, Bishop Robert Morneau of the diocese of Green Bay, Wisconsin delivered an inspirational message in his typically low-key, understated, and poetic style. The next day, Jesuit Father J-Glenn Murray whipped the crowd into a frenzy with his stories and his spontaneous renditions of African-American spirituals. *Both* were passionate. *Both* proclaimed the good news of Jesus' resurrection. One did it quietly; the other with flare. The crowds that came to hear their message left *both* days with the same conclusion. It was the same message that the two disciples formerly on the road to Emmaus came away with when they returned to their fellow disciples in Jerusalem: "The Lord has truly been raised!"

In our own ministry, we develop a style of proclaiming the risen Christ to others. Some of us may express our joy very openly and with great fanfare. Many of us will do it in a quiet and understated manner. Pope Paul VI emphasized just how important this quiet witness is: "Through this wordless witness . . . Christians stir up irresistible questions in the hearts of those who see how they live: Why are they like this? Why do they live this way? What or who is it that inspires them? Why are they in our midst? Such a witness is already a silent proclamation of the good news and a very powerful and effective one."[33]

To be renewed and to be set on fire with passion for the Lord Jesus Christ does not mean that we have to make a lot of noise. St. Paul warned about noisy gongs and clanging cymbals. Those of us who are of the quieter variety need to remember that even the biggest fires begin with a small flicker of a flame that will eventually ignite everything around it. The important thing is that we spread the good news with energy and enthusiasm, whether with fanfare or in quiet, subtle ways.

Where is the Hope?

If we truly listen to the Lord and allow him to open our eyes to see in a whole new way, our own personal journeys to Emmaus will eventually lead us back to Jerusalem. Upon their return, the two disciples of Emmaus fame were met with affirmation of their own encounter with the risen Lord. They entered into the midst of their brothers and sisters to the sounds of "The Lord has truly been raised!" They encountered signs of hope that affirmed their belief that Jesus had indeed been in their midst and that they were truly reborn.

We, too, need to look and listen for these signs of hope in our midst. All around us, we can find signs of hope in the resurrection of Jesus if we only tune our eyes and ears to see and hear them—and tune out the deafening sounds of cynicism and negativity. We minister in a world that is asking the question: Where is the hope? We need to search for signs of hope for ourselves so that we, in turn, can proclaim hope to others. Through our actions and sometimes even our words, we will be able to proclaim that *Jesus* is the hope!

Often in my ministry, when I gather with fellow Christians and I keep quiet long enough to listen to them tell their story, I am overwhelmed and inspired by their deep faith. When I listen to people share their faith in the risen Lord, my eyes are opened to signs of hope right in my midst. It turns out to be those *to whom* I am ministering who reveal to me what faith is really all about as they express their trust in the transforming power of the risen Lord. One of the ways we can renew our ministry is to allow ourselves to be renewed by the faith of those to whom we are called to serve. As we move ahead in our journey of faith, you and I need to be on the lookout for signs of hope: in our Church, with our local faith community, among our colleagues, and most of all, among those we serve. Like the disciples on the road, we need to hear others proclaim, "The Lord has truly been raised!" so that we, in turn, can be inspired to recount our own experiences of encountering the risen Christ.

Have No Fear

Although the Emmaus story does not include the words "do not be afraid" or "have no fear," it is obvious from the passage that the two disciples indeed had no fear after their encounter with Jesus. Previously, everything blinded them with fear and despair. Now, after encountering Jesus, their eyes were opened to recognize the One who brings peace and dispels darkness and fear. Their return to Jerusalem and their eagerness to tell their story reveals an amazing lack of fear that seems to be the result of their transforming encounter with the risen Lord.

In almost every other resurrection narrative, some words aimed at calming fear are uttered either by Jesus or by the angels to those who encounter the risen Christ or come upon the empty tomb:

- "Do not be afraid! I know that you are seeking Jesus the crucified" (Mt 28:5).
- "Do not be afraid. Go tell my brothers to go to Galilee, and there they will see me" (Mt 28:10).
- "Do not be amazed! You seek Jesus of Nazareth, the crucified. He has been raised" (Mk 16:6).
- "Peace be with you. Why are you troubled?" (Lk 24:36,38).
- "Peace be with you" (Jn 20:19).

In order for us to recount *our* story, we, too, must be at peace. We must be in a state of *shalom*, meaning that we are without fear and anxiety. We must be full of confidence that the risen Lord is in our midst. St. Teresa of Jesus eloquently describes the calming effect of true faith:

Let nothing trouble you / Let nothing frighten you
Everything passes / God never changes
Patience / Obtains all

Whoever has God / Wants for nothing
God alone is enough.[34]

Go Tell It on the Mountain

Armed with the confidence that the risen Jesus brings to us,
we, too, are able to leave behind our fears and anxieties and go
forth to proclaim good news. The two disciples did not remain in
Emmaus selfishly basking in the glow of their spiritual experience,
but instead returned to the scene of the crime (literally) where
they now recognized signs of hope and discovered the energy and
boldness they needed to recount their story.

Each day, as we get out of bed and prepare for another day of
ministry, we need to remind ourselves that in all we do and say, we
are being sent forth to proclaim this hope to the world. Whether
we are:

- preparing for a parish meeting
- typing notes for a presentation
- calling on the phone for volunteers
- visiting the sick
- printing and mailing a parish newsletter
- filing parish records
- preparing our next religious education lesson
- balancing our program's checkbook
- presiding over a liturgical gathering
- rehearsing a reading for our next turn on the lector
  schedule
- keyboarding next week's bulletin announcements.

We need to remind ourselves that we are doing so because
we have seen the risen Lord and, in whatever way possible, we
want to tell this to others. Not even the smallest and most
insignificant part of our ministry is meaningless when we know
that it is in some way assisting disciples of Jesus to "*Go*, tell it on
the mountain!"

Recounting our story is what disciples of Christ do. It is interesting to note that in the gospels, we do not have any narratives of
the resurrection. John Shea reminds us that "The Resurrection of

Jesus is confessed but not narrated. We have stories about an empty tomb; but we have no eyewitness accounts of Jesus' coming back to life."[35] It is up to us to continue telling the story of how we have come to know Jesus on the road and in the breaking of the bread. To quote the old Negro spiritual: "Go, tell it on the mountain! Over the hills and everywhere!"

To Teach as Jesus Did

In his apostolic exhortation *Evangelii Nuntiandi*, Pope Paul VI shared a remarkably true statement: "The person who has been evangelized goes on to evangelize others. Here lies the test of truth, the touchstone of evangelization; it is unthinkable that a person should accept the Word and give himself to the Kingdom without becoming a person who bears witness to it and proclaims it in his turn."[36] How true this is. The Emmaus story illustrates this beautifully by showing us how the disciples are evangelized by the Word and then become witnesses to it, returning to Jerusalem to recount their story.

As pastoral ministers, you are called to be evangelized and to evangelize others. As a result of this dynamic, the "student" becomes the "teacher" and the cycle begins all over again. The *General Directory for Catechesis* reminds us that evangelization then gives birth to the ministry of catechesis, that is the re-sounding (recounting) of God's Word. No sooner do we hear the Word proclaimed to us than we are compelled to proclaim it and explain it to others. This means that all of us have a role in the ministry of *evangelization* as well as a role in the ministry of *catechesis*.

Catechesis is not something that only directors of religious education do, nor is it something that only refers to teaching religion to children in grades K-8 (what we formerly called CCD). Catechesis refers to all of the efforts through which the church attempts to shape the vision of those who call themselves disciples of Christ in order to "put people not only in touch, but also in communion and intimacy with Jesus Christ."

The *General Directory for Catechesis* continues this explanation of evangelization and catechesis: "Both activities are essential and mutually complementary: go and welcome, proclaim and educate, call and incorporate . . . in pastoral practice it is not always easy to define the boundaries of these activities. Catechesis is one of these moments—a very remarkable one—in the whole process of evangelization."[37] Through all of our efforts, we are attempting to open the eyes of would-be disciples of Christ in the same manner that our own eyes were once opened. Just as Jesus walked with the disciples on the road, all of Jesus' disciples must, in turn, walk the road with others, listen, challenge, offer perspective, show hospitality and break bread so that soon, the whole world may see that Jesus is Lord!

Making Disciples: The Art of Apprenticeship

All of this leads us to a most essential point: renewal in ministry necessitates a replenishment of ministers. The two disciples on the road returned to Jerusalem to recount their story. However, they did not simply pass the story around in a small clique. Luke tells us in his "sequel," the Acts of the Apostles, that when the feast of Pentecost arrived, the disciples left the seclusion of their upper room, filled with the Holy Spirit, and recounted their story in the streets of Jerusalem to people from all nations. Within hours, their numbers increased by three thousand and the growth of the gospel began in earnest.

Luke further tells us that these new disciples "devoted themselves to the teaching of the apostles" (Acts 2:42) or as we refer to it today, *catechesis*. Acts goes on to say that "every day the Lord added to their number" (2:47). Within days, there arose a need for assistants (Acts 6:1) in order to carry out the ministry. Seven were chosen and we are told, "the word of God continued to spread, and the number of the disciples in Jerusalem increased greatly," (Acts 6:7). It seems that the early church had developed the fine art of "apprenticeship!"

The word *apprentice* is not used as much today as it once was. In my own life, I was lucky enough to have an experience of apprenticeship. Growing up in a family that owned a pharmacy required that I, along with my eight brothers and sisters, help out in the store after school, on weekends, and during the summer. When I reached legal age, my dad had me apply for what was then called a "Pharmacy Apprentice License," giving me the authority to legally assist him in filling prescriptions under his watchful eye. This experience of being apprenticed by my dad and then by my uncle, who was also a pharmacist, taught me a great lesson in how to organize a business and serve customers. Though I did not go into pharmacy (my close call with Phar-Mor notwithstanding), that apprenticeship taught me skills that I continue to use today in order to serve others.

If our ministry and our church are to truly be renewed, we need to begin apprenticing others to follow in our footsteps. We need to encourage others to assume the task of proclaiming the gospel under our watchful eye. The *General Directory for Catechesis* actually uses the word apprenticeship in describing this task: "Christian community life is not realized spontaneously. It is necessary to educate it carefully. In this apprenticeship, the teaching of Christ on community life . . . calls for attitudes which it is for catechesis to inculcate."[38] Upon our return from Emmaus, we are called, like the two disciples, to recount our story of how we have encountered the risen Christ so that others may come to know him in the breaking of bread.

Knowing Jesus, Making Jesus Known

We have covered a lot of ground on this journey that took us to Emmaus and back again. Ministry is not easy. We experience many detours, bumps-in-the-road, head-on collisions, and engine failures. Through it all, however, we can rely on one thing: the risen Lord who is at our side at all times. The Emmaus story tells us that when the disciples recounted their story, they told about how they came to *know* Jesus in the breaking of the bread. Until that time, they had only *known about* Jesus. Their earlier discussion on the road reveals that they had all kinds of hopes and expectations about Jesus and knew all about his miraculous ministry. Up to this point, however, they did not personally *know* Jesus.

If we are truly to renew our ministry, we must get to know Jesus—personally and intimately. Jesus is the one who brought renewal to the two disciples on the road to Emmaus. In their time together, the disciples opened up and allowed Jesus to enter into their vulnerability where true knowing takes place. As ministers and followers of Jesus, we too must open ourselves up and allow Jesus to enter into our vulnerability. Then and only then can we let go of all the things that prevent us from holding on to Jesus. Then and only then can we come to see that Jesus alone sustains us and transforms us. Then and only then will our eyes be opened so that we, too, can recognize the presence of the risen Lord who fills us with new life, renews and energizes us, and sends us "on the road again" to recount our story and make disciples of all nations.

> *Now this is eternal life, that they should know*
> *you, the only true God, and the one whom you*
> *sent, Jesus Christ.*

—John 17:3

QUESTIONS FOR REFLECTION

- Who proclaims the message, "The Lord has truly been raised!" to you? How do you proclaim this message to others?
- Where do you see signs of hope and new life around you?
- When was a time that your faith was renewed by someone you were ministering to?
- In what area of your ministry do you need the risen Lord to dispel all fear?
- What are the tedious parts of your ministry? How can these still be seen as working toward the spread of the good news?
- In your ministry, how do you both *evangelize* (welcome and proclaim) and *catechize* (proclaim and educate)?
- Who "apprenticed" you into the ministry? Who are you apprenticing?
- What can you do to get to know Jesus better?

INSIGHT

And then Easter happened. Jesus rose from the dead. The incredible, the unexpected happened. Life triumphed over death, light over darkness, love over hatred, good over evil. That is what Easter means—hope prevails over despair. Jesus reigns as Lord of Lords and King of Kings. Oppression and injustice and suffering can't be the end of the human story. Freedom and justice, peace and reconciliation, are his will for all of us... in this land and throughout the world. Easter says to us that despite everything to the contrary, his will for us will prevail, love will prevail over hate, justice over injustice and oppression, peace over exploitation and bitterness. The Lord is risen! Alleluia!

—Bishop Desmond Tutu[39]

SCRIPTURE FOR PRAYER

The stone which the builders rejected
has become the cornerstone.
By the Lord has this been done;
it is wonderful in our eyes.
This is the day the Lord has made;
let us rejoice in it and be glad.
Lord, grant salvation!
Lord, grant good fortune!

—Psalm 118:22-25

Epilogue
The Emmaus Story as a Template for Ministry

The 3 E's

Up until this time, we have been reflecting upon the Emmaus story by focusing on the two disciples and how they were renewed and energized with new vision for their ministry by the risen Christ. I believe that this approach is a prerequisite to reflecting upon the Emmaus story from Jesus' perspective. Before we can hope to imitate the Master, we need to embrace the role of disciple. Once we have journeyed to Emmaus and allowed the Lord to open our eyes to a new way of seeing, we are ready to turn around and invite others to walk the road with us. The Emmaus story unfolds in such a manner that it provides a template or framework of guiding principles for our ministry, whatever that may be. If we are truly to be disciples of Jesus, then we should minister as Jesus did. The Emmaus model of ministry lays out three basic steps to approaching any ministerial situation. I will call these the "3 E's": Empathy, Equip, and Exit.

Empathy

The first rule for ministry is to shift attention away from ourselves and onto those we are called to serve. The Emmaus story reveals to us that Jesus sought out the two disciples on the road to Emmaus. He was in search of those who needed healing. Ministry is not about us, it is about those in need and how the saving power of Jesus can enter into, fill, and transform their lives and needs.

Like the crew of the *Starship Enterprise* from *Star Trek*, we are on a mission to seek out new life. Jesus not only sought out the two disciples on the road, but he then proceeded to inquire about their needs with questions like: "What are you discussing as you walk along?" and "What sort of things?" Jesus knew full well what was in their minds and hearts but he created an environment of empathy by inviting them to speak. Jesus then did a very important thing: *he listened.* Although he was the main character of the story they were relating, he patiently listened as they spoke. Jesus could have saved a great deal of time if he skipped to the "Oh, how foolish you are!" part of the discussion. Instead, he established a relationship by listening; something that validates the experience of others.

In our own ministry, we are often too quick to begin providing solutions for people before we have even listened to their stories and assessed their needs. We are eager to implement our ministerial programs before we have "kissed the soil" of our new environment in the tradition of Pope John Paul II upon arriving in a country for the first time. Even though we may indeed have a clear vision for how the ministry should be implemented in whatever environment we have been called to, if we take the time to gather people first and ask them what they are "discussing" or concerned with, we metaphorically kiss the soil upon which they have tread and upon which we have been invited to walk along with them. This kind of empathy shows a deep respect for the experience of those we are called to serve, even if we are eventually called to challenge that experience.

One other point to focus on in reference to empathy is the fact that the two disciples did not recognize Jesus at once. This suggests that Jesus was not drawing attention to himself. He could have jumped in front of them and announced with a flare, "Hey, it's me!" Instead, he holds back and focuses on them. In our own ministry, we need to be more invisible. Ministry is not about directing attention to us but about focusing on others. When we minister, we should be transparent enough for people to see through us to the saving presence of Jesus. When we offer the gift of empathy, we meet others on their turf and walk with them until they can recognize that Jesus has been with them throughout the journey.

Equip

Only after listening does Jesus open his mouth to propose another way of thinking. By empathizing with the two disciples, Jesus validates their experience and indeed, their very being. He may not have agreed with their point of view, but he earned their respect—something that would soon allow him to challenge them. Jesus can utter the words, "Oh, how foolish you are!" only because he first listened.

Knowing what the disciples needed and having listened to them verbalize it, Jesus then set out to equip them with a new set of eyes. He does this in two ways: he challenges them and he catechizes them. Jesus' choice of "Oh, how foolish you are!" is a way of jolting the disciples into the realization that they are in need of change. Empathy does not mean that we have to agree with someone, only that we respect them enough to listen and then offer an alternative. Oftentimes, people need to be called to change. They may realize that all is not well with their lives, but all they can do is continually re-visit the pain and frustration. It is our responsibility as ministers to be sure that people realize there are other ways of seeing reality, ways that replace our foolish ways and lead to new life.

After this challenge, however, Jesus does not say "good luck" and walk away. I know of several pastoral ministers who seem to enjoy showing up at various ministerial functions in order to "drop bombs" (e.g., they offer stinging criticism about how everyone else is missing the mark with their ministry) and then leave. Jesus not only challenges, but he also *equips* his disciples with the knowledge they need to alter their vision. Catechesis is the tool we use to equip people with the knowledge and skills they need to place their personal story within a greater framework; namely the story of our salvation in Christ Jesus. Without catechesis, we are doing a disservice to those we evangelize. Catechesis is to evangelization as watering is to planting seeds. If we are truly calling people to a new way of seeing and living, we owe it to them to equip them with the knowledge and skills needed to foster their ongoing conversion.

We need to offer catechesis, not just to our grade school children, but also to our parish pastoral councils, our high school and college students, our liturgical ministers, our mother's and father's clubs, our Holy Name Societies and Knights of Columbus, our parents preparing a child to receive one of the sacraments, and all those we serve. Then and only then can we truly say that we are equipping others with the knowledge and skills needed to transform their lives and the world.

Finally, Jesus not only provided a challenge followed by some catechesis, he provided his disciples with food for the journey. Jesus gave us the eucharist so that we would never again be left alone. In all of our ministerial efforts, we need to be sure that we are ultimately leading people to the table where they will be fed with food for their journey. Likewise, we need to be sure that we are paying attention to our liturgical ministries so that our eucharistic meals truly equip and nourish those who gather to partake. As I mentioned in my previous work, *YOU Give Them Something to Eat* (Ave Maria Press, 1998), there is no such thing as "fast food" when it comes to the church. Our liturgies must indeed be banquets!

Exit

Remember the puzzling passage in the Emmaus story in which Jesus vanishes from their sight? Jesus knew full well that in order for his two disciples to fully realize their potential, they had to stand on their own four feet! Jesus vanishes, yet he remains present. This scene is reminiscent of something the gospel of John quotes Jesus as saying: "I tell you the truth, it is better for you that I go. For if I do not go, the Advocate will not come to you. But if I go, I will send him to you" (16:7).

Jesus was able to let go and allow the disciples to take over the reins. He was able to allow the students to become the teacher. In our own ministry, we must also learn to do the same. We need to equip people and then enable them by "exiting." John the Baptist knew when it was time to step aside after preparing the way for Jesus: "He must increase; I must decrease," John said (Jn 3:30).

As pastoral ministers, we are not called to be the "jack-of-all trades," although many of us can and do wear many hats. Our job is not to do all the work, but to enable others to do so. We must invite others, equip them, and then exit or step aside, allowing them to carry the word of God to others. This requires great trust. However, if the Lord could entrust his message to us, should we not do the same by trusting others?

And where does that exit lead? Back on to the road again where we encounter the risen Christ. It is he who opens our eyes so that we may continue to minister with renewed energy and vision.

> *May God inspire you to follow the example of the apostles,*
> *and give witness to the truth before all.*
>
> —*The Sacramentary*, Solemn Blessing, Apostles

Acknowledgments

1. From *No Man Is An Island* by Thomas Merton (New York: Harvest/HBJ, 1978), p. 232.

2. From *Mother Teresa of Calcutta* ed. by George Gorree and Jean Barbier (San Francisco: Harper & Row, 1982), pp. 109-110.

3. From *St. Francis of Assisi* by Thomas of Celano (Chicago: Franciscan Herald Press, 1963), p. 240.

4. The information on Dr. Elisabeth Kubler-Ross's stages of the grieving process was taken from *On Death and Dying* (New York: Macmillan Publishing Co., 1969).

5. From *The Great Themes of Scripture: Old Testament* by Richard Rohr and Joseph Martos (Cincinnati: St. Anthony Messenger Press, 1987)p. 67.

6. The quotation by Dr. Elizabeth Kubler-Ross is found on page 140 of *On Death and Dying*.

7. From *Reconstructing Catholicism: For A New Generation* by Dr. Robert Ludwig (New York: Crossroads, 1995), pp. 3-4.

8. From "Letter from a Birmingham Jail" by Martin Luther King, Jr. quoted in *A Testament of Hope* edited by James Melvin Washington (San Francisco: Harper and Row, 1986), pp. 299-300.

9. From *The Skilled Helper* by Gerard Egan (Monterey, CA: Brooks/Cole, 1982), p. 186.

10. Ibid.

11. From *The Three Ways of the Spiritual Life* by R. Girrigou-LaGrange, O.P. (Rockford, IL: Tan, 1977), p. 46.

12. The definition of *metanoia* is taken from *The New World Dictionary Concordance of the New American Bible* (Iowa Falls, IA: World Bible Publishing, Co., 1984), p. 521.

13. The story "Letting Go of the Mountain" is taken from *Handbook for the Soul* by Benjamin Shield, Ph.D. (New York: Little, Brown & Co., 1995), p. 169.

14. From *Christotherapy II* by Bernard Tyrell (New York: Paulist Press, 1982), p. 216.

15. From *Redemptive Intimacy* by Dick Westley (Mystic, CT: Twenty Third Publications, 1981), p. 124.

16. From *The Gospel According to Luke, The New Jerome Biblical Commentary* by Robert J. Karris (Englewood Cliffs, NJ: Prentice-Hall, 1990), p. 721.

17. The story of the exchange between Peter and Jesus is quoted from *An Experience Named Spirit* by John Shea (Allen, TX: Thomas More, 1983), pp. 213-214.

18. From *The Resurrection According to Matthew, Mark and Luke* by Norman Perrin (Philadelphia: Fortress Press, 1977), p. 65.

19. The quotation by Soren Kierkegaard is from *Redemptive Intimacy* by Dick Westley (Mystic, CT: Twenty Third Publications, 1981), p. 103.

20. From *St. Paul* by Rea McDonnell, S.S.N.D. (Boston: Pauline Books and Media, 1998), p. 13.

21. The descriptions of ministry "burnout" are taken from *Ministry Burnout* by John Sanford (New York: Paulist Press, 1982), p. 4.

22. From the article "Passion and Soulfulness" by Nathaniel Branden quoted in *Handbook for the Soul* edited by Richard Carlson and Benjamin Shield (Boston: Little, Brown & Co., 1995), p. 99.

23. From *The Seven Habits of Highly Effective People* (New York: Fireside, 1989) by Steven Covey, pp. 43-54.

24. From *Who Has Seen the Wind?* by Louis Savary, S.J. (New York: Regina Press, 1976), p. 58.

25. From St. John of the Cross, *The Dark Night*, bk II, ch. 10, in *The Collected Works of St. John of the Cross*, trans. by K. Kavanaugh, O.C.D. and O. Rodriguez, O.C.D. (Washington, D.C.: ICS, 1973) p. 350.

26. From *Passion For Excellence* by Tom Peters and Nancy Austin (New York: Warner Books, 1985), pp. 140, 160, 179.

27. *The Seven Habits of Highly Effective People* by Stephen Covey (New York: Fireside, 1989), p. 70.

28. From *Evangelii Nuntiandi* (Washington, DC: United States Catholic Conference, 1975), #80.

29. From *The Seven Habits of Highly Effective People* by Stephen Covey (New York: Fireside, 1989), pp. 106-107.

30. From *Redemptive Intimacy* by Dick Westley (Mystic, CT: Twenty-Third Publications, 1981), p. 92.

31. From *Spiritual Passages* by Benedict Groeschel (New York: Crossroad, 1984), p. 122.

32. From *Radical Grace* by Richard Rohr (Cincinnati: St. Anthony Messenger Press, 1993), p. 320.

33. From Pope Paul VI as quoted in *The Spirit Master* by John Shea (Chicago: Thomas More Press, 1987), p. 25.

34. The excerpt by St. Teresa of Jesus is taken from the *Catechism of the Catholic Church*, Liberia Editrice Vaticana (Washington, DC: USCC, 1994), #227.

35. From *The Spirit Master* by John Shea (Chicago: Thomas More Press, 1987), pp. 66-67.

36. From *Evangelii Nuntiandi* (Washington, DC: United States Catholic Conference, 1975), #24.

37. These citations and quotations are from the *General Directory for Catechesis* (Washington, DC: USCC, 1997), #61-63.

38. From the *General Directory for Catechesis* (Washington, DC: USCC, 1997), #86a.

39. From the sermon "An Easter Message" by Bishop Desmond Tutu quoted in *An Invitation to Christian Spirituality: An Ecumenical Anthology* (New York: Oxford University Press, 1999) p. 460.